Social Media in
Social Work Education

 Editor: Joanne Westwood

First published in 2014 by Critical Publishing Ltd.

British Library Cataloguing in Publication Data
A CIP record for this book is available from the British Library

ISBN: 978-1-909682-57-3

This book is also available in the following e-book formats:
MOBI ISBN: 978-1-909682-58-0
EPUB ISBN: 978-1-909682-59-7
Adobe e-book ISBN: 978-1-909682-60-3

Cover design by Greensplash Limited
Project Management by Out of House Publishing
Typeset by Newgen Knowledge Works Pvt Ltd.
Printed and bound in Great Britain by Bell & Bain, Glasgow

Critical Publishing
152 Chester Road
Northwich
CW8 4AL
www.criticalpublishing.com

Contents

List of illustrations

FIGURE

TABLES

BOXES

Meet the authors

Tarsem Singh Cooner @Alkali

Tarsem is an Associate Director of CEIMH at Birmingham University where he is a lecturer in social work. Tarsem has used Facebook to teach students about professionalism and social media. His research interests include the use of mobile technologies in professional education. He recently published the Social Work Social Media mobile app. Tarsem has received several awards in recognition of his contributions to teaching and learning in higher education.

David McKendrick @bonkelsoul

David is a lecturer in social work at Glasgow Caledonian University. He is interested in using Social Media to support a range of teaching and learning activities. Most recently he established the Twitter chat @swinduction an online forum that supports students making the transition to studying social work at university.

Jackie Rafferty @Jaxrafferty

Jackie Rafferty held a professorial level director role at the University of Southampton before she retired in 2012. As Director of the Centre for Human Service Technology and the Higher Education Academy Subject Centre for Social Policy and Social Work she has been involved with the use of technology in social work education and practice since 1989. Currently Jackie is helping the Joint University Council–Social Work Education Committee to communicate with its members through technology and is on the planning group of the Joint Social Work Education Conference.

Amanda Taylor @AMLTaylor

Amanda is a Senior Lecturer in the School of Social Work at the University of Central Lancashire. Amanda's previous employment was as a social worker in the fields of psychiatry, mental health and deafness and as a specialist social worker for children with various degrees of deafness; all set within the Northern Ireland Integrative Health and Social Care Structure. Amanda has been nominated and won a number of teaching and learning awards for her teaching innovation and is well known for the development of a National Book Group.

Liz Thackray @lizith

Liz Thackray was employed for nearly 20 years as a social worker and manager in both voluntary and statutory settings before taking a career break and retraining in information systems. She became interested in the uses of social media when working as an e-learning consultant with the Sussex Learning Network. Liz recently completed her PhD at the University of Sussex, where her research explored problematic aspects of the special needs domain and the use of systems approaches as a research framework.

Denise Turner @DeniseT01

Denise Turner is a former social worker and a Lecturer in the Department of Social Work and Social Care at the University of Sussex. Her PhD research concerned parents' experience of professional interventions following sudden, unexpected child death. On-going research includes professional narrative accounts of involvement with sudden, unexpected child death; autoethnography and methodological innovation; psychosocial perspectives; 'sensitive' and 'taboo' topics; and the provision of death education and training. Denise is interested in how academics, practitioners, and service users can be encouraged to support and learn from each other and her interest in social media stems from a drive to build communities of practice which nurture and sustain.

Joanne Westwood @jlwestwood

Joanne trained and worked as a social worker in statutory and voluntary/community sectors. Joanne teaches child welfare, childhood theory, and communication and interpersonal skills. Joanne was awarded her PhD in 2010 and she undertakes research in social media as a tool for teaching and learning in higher education and research related to the promotion of children and young people's participation and their welfare. Joanne is a co-director of the Centre for Children and Young People's Participation based at the University of Central Lancashire.

Foreword

It is a real pleasure for me to welcome you to writing which will stimulate –whether you are an educator, practitioner, or student. It's only very recently that social media has started to have an impact on social work education and this book makes a timely contribution to these developments. It signals a sea change in how we utilise the benefits of social media and learning technologies more widely in social work education and in practice.

'*Social work is about people not computers.*' This is an accurate statement but sometimes it can be the technology that brings people together. At the Joint Social Work Education Conference (JSWEC) in Manchester in 2011 I thought I might be the only person tweeting from the conference but there were two others; @georgejulian, whom I had never met, and @markwatsonCK whom I had known since the 1990s. Mark knew George and pointed her out to me, we made face to face contact and now have a relationship that enriches me both professionally and personally but is mainly through Twitter.

At JSWEC 2012 Jon Bolton put together a list of people on Twitter talking from and about the conference www.twitter.com/jonbolton/tweeters-at-jswec-2012/members 52 in total: professors, lecturers, practitioners, policy people, publishers, journalists, students, and service users. But it was also at this conference that during one workshop the proceedings were stopped by someone who objected to my rudeness of using a smartphone whilst the speaker was talking. I was tweeting the speaker's key ideas to those who were unable to participate physically in the conference. If I remember correctly this was in a session about the use of technology in social work education, led by Tarsem Singh Cooner, one of the contributors to this book. Whereas in 2011 using technology to disseminate knowledge 'on the fly' was so unfamiliar, and such a minority activity, nobody noticed; by 2012 the growth of the use of social media use within the conference challenged the traditional norms.

It was also at the 2011 and 2012 conferences that I met face to face for the first time with people I had been communicating with on Twitter: Amanda Taylor, Joanne Westwood, and Jon Bolton. Were you there too David McKendrick? It was from these conferences and subsequent discussions on Twitter that the idea of a keynote on social work and social media for the 2013 JSWEC conference was born. It was time to come out as social work educators who use social media. The introduction to the book will talk about this birth in greater detail. I think the keynote in 2013 and this subsequent book marks a new epoch in the use of technology in social work education. It has been a very long time coming.

In 1989 I was working on a nationally funded project, the Computers in Teaching Initiative (CTI).[1] My job was to find out what technology was being used in higher education and in social work and travel the length and breadth of the United Kingdom persuading social work educators that this 'new' technology was to be taken seriously and needed to be embedded in social work student learning.

I started by finding out what was going on in the world of the use of technology in higher education: a whole alphabet soup of policies, projects, and initiatives. Discussion and debate as to whether CBT (Computer Based Training) was passé and CBL was the name of the game (Computer Based Learning) or whether we should be moving on to emphasise the computer less and the learning more (e-learning), and, was that with or without a hyphen? At the same time I researched where technology was being used in social work practice.

There were clunky 'client' information systems in local authorities but where were the exciting innovative empowering uses? There were a few: the Women's Institute group in rural mid Wales using UseNet and GreenNet to comment on UN policies on women; the two ex-Citizen Advice Bureau advisers who set up a company in 1987 and developed a Psion based welfare benefits calculation system, still trading 22 years later as Ferret Information Systems[2] (at that time social work qualifying courses still taught welfare benefits).

The CTI Centre for Human Services, set up a website, held a database of resources, ran workshops, visited universities, published a journal, wrote papers and newsletters, brokered and networked. The Centre ran for ten years and was independently evaluated in 1994 and 1999 as highly successful, but my own evaluation was that in terms of embedded change not so much had happened. We were going around with a near empty shopping bag, there was very little in the way of e-learning resources that were social work curriculum specific. So we started to develop materials under another acronym'd initiative: TLTP – Technology Learning and Teaching Programme. We developed materials on *Interpersonal Communications* and *Research Mindedness*, firstly on 3.5" floppy disks, then CDs and finally the web. But, for all the talk in higher education, the infrastructure and teaching approaches had not as yet caught up. We found one university where, in 1997, the only computers were a small collection of Amstrads, Apricots, and BBC microcomputers in a basement room half a mile across campus from where the social work students were.

With the advent of the Web and the realisation that source material could be accessed there was a move to the notion of RBL (Resource Based Learning) which paired better with the constructivist pedagogic model that was gaining ground, variously called RBL or Enquiry Based Learning or Problem Based Learning. There was an underpinning assumption that learning through technology would be cheaper than traditional ways of learning. Much money was spent to prove it, and when they couldn't, to examine how they could. It was all about content at that time, interactivity was claimed if the learner was asked a question onscreen and had the opportunity to select from a multiple choice answer. I know because we did that too. Some social work educators were using e-resources as a bolt on, or replacement, for what they had always done. E-learning is a

---

[1] An evaluation of the CTI is still accessible Higher Education Funding Council.
[2] Ferret Information Systems – www.ferret.co.uk.

Trojan horse. To use it effectively you have to deconstruct what you are doing and rethink it. It was a natural progression for us, to work on the whole approach to learning, not just that part that is supported by technology, thus the rationale for bidding for the Centre that has come to an end after 11 years, the Higher Education Academy for Social Work and Social Policy (SWAP) which started in 2000.[3]

In 2003 the old 'new social work degree' came into being. The Department of Health with other key stakeholders looked at what was happening in allied qualifying professional programmes and discovered that Nurses had to gain the European Computer Driving Licence (ECDL).[4] I got invited to the meeting that talked about making ECDL a requirement in social work education and argued that learning to word process, develop a spread sheet and a database were not sufficient. I lost. My one claim to fame is that during the Social Work Reform Board process I wrote the position paper that supported the decision to drop the ECDL requirement in 2010. It was hugely time consuming, expensive, mechanistic and there were fraught issues to do with what happened if you didn't pass all the modules, did that mean you could not become a qualified social worker?

Yet 2003 was the first time that there was some recognition that technology skills were needed in social work education and practice. And this is the crux of this piece which I have taken a long time to get to. There is a disjointedness between the energy and effort that is being expended in higher education on using technology to 'transform' the learning experience (another phrase we will live to regret no doubt); the technology skills that employers say they want from social workers (ie word processing and how to use the complex relational database that holds service user, monitoring and audit information); and what I think is needed: which is to mirror in social work skills and understanding the reality of the use of technology in the world we now live in.

So we need to differentiate and expand our thinking from technology skills for learning and employment: ie how to word process, search the web, use PowerPoint, use databases and spread sheets; through where I think we are now with a focus on digital literacy (the ability to locate, organise, understand, evaluate, analyse, and reflect on information and knowledge using digital technology) to having the skills and being able to understand the opportunities and risks of engaging as social worker practitioners, students, and educators, with society: including communities, service users, other professionals, managers, and policy makers; through multiple channels of communication.

We still need content but communication and collaboration is to the fore and I now use social media tools such as Twitter and Facebook, to share information; to ask others' opinions; to find out information and facts; to say what I think and to see what others are thinking; to find like-minded people and contrary minded people; to reflect and to develop and test ideas and to work together. The focus is on relationship and trust building. I am delighted to be tangentially involved with this book and its authors as they are playing my type of music and taking forward ideas in to substantive change in the ways technology can support social work learning.

Jackie Rafferty @jaxrafferty

---

[3] Higher Education Academy for Social Work and Social Policy – www.swap.ac.uk.
[4] European Computer Driving Licence – www.ecdl.com.

Acknowledgements

We would like to express our very great thanks to the social work academics, practitioners, and the willing and eager social work students who we have worked with on the projects discussed in this book. Social media is a new area of research in our profession and we are grateful for the support we have received from our institutions and from our families and friends which has enabled us to bring our interests together in this volume. Specifically we would like to thank the very many people out there in our social media networks who have contributed to our thinking, shared their resources, expertise, and ideas with us and been with us on this journey. We hope that the materials and resources we identify and discuss here assist educators, students and practitioners in their work and stimulate creative approaches to using social media and learning technologies further.

Introduction

Joanne Westwood

WHAT IS THIS BOOK ABOUT?

Why a book about social media in social work education? The aim of this book is to bring together some important work which has been developed and already has an impact on social work education. Many of us, whether educators, practitioner, or students, use social media to connect with our friends, peers, colleagues, and our families. Harnessing the benefits of social media in an educational context brings many challenges and the authors of the chapters in this book have already begun to grapple with these and find solutions to them. How can you use Facebook safely with students to encourage them to critically reflect on their values and inform their intervention? What contributions does blogging make to social work education and how can writing a blog contribute to your own academic writing? What barriers are there for students to use social media in their learning journey? The projects discussed in this book illustrate creative approaches to social work education which provide the flexibility and accessibility which students require.

WHO IS THIS BOOK FOR?

We believe that developing a professional profile, interacting, networking, and collaborating with fellow students is a key aspect of social work education which can be developed and enhanced through the sensitive and informed use of social media. Student social workers may recognise some of the barriers to their engaging in social media and realise that there are many ways in which their engagement can complement and enhance their learning experience. Approaches which are being used in social word education include blogging, the Social work Social Media App (www.youtube.com/watch?v=_Vr6BLGdLcs), Twitter debates and discussions for example @swinduction, @swchat, and @SWBookGroup. Students are also using social media as a way of sharing their learning journey and making connections with like-minded people and organisations. Manisha Patel (@ManishaMahen) is a student social worker who is interested in the issues related to human trafficking and posts regular tweets about this. Manisha also shares her feelings about her experiences as a social work student using Twitter and a blog.

Social work practitioners may find that engaging with social media provides them with useful ways to keep their theory updated and facilitates their access to and participation in discussions with prominent social work academics and educators/trainers. Some key social work theorists and writers participate in Twitter discussions. Several of these academics post their views or re tweet other tweets on political events related to social work, including Claudia Bernard (@DrCBernard) whose profile states: '*Social work academic, interested in black feminist thinking, critical race theory, gender-based violence.*' Another tweep is Peter Beresford (@BeresfordPeter) whose profile states that he is a service user activist concerned with mental health, disability, welfare issues, and committed to participation. Brid Featherstone (@Brigid39), who was recently appointed Chair of the Children and Families Faculty at The College, is a social work professor at the Open University and undertakes research on gender and inequalities. He is also a regular tweep. These and many other social work academics in the United Kingdom and beyond maintain a social media presence and use social media as a way of expressing their views and opinions and to engage in debates, discussion and make connections.

@BASW_UK which is the official Twitter feed for the British Association of Social Workers publicises policy and practice issues on Twitter, as well as news and reports on social work issues and links to enable speedy access to these. Social media also includes professional networks and associations which engage and facilitate real time collaborations. The Social Care Curry Club (@SocialCareCurry) which was featured in a national newspaper was established through a discussion on Twitter:

> Earlier this year a chance conversation on Twitter led to the most unusual of networks forming, the Social Care Curry Club. Variously billed as edible networking, curry induced knowledge exchange, and a good excuse to eat curry and chat social care, the appetite for curry has surpassed all expectations.
>
> (The Guardian 2013)

Social work practice educators may find valuable and immediate links to new developments in training, as well as access to free online resources promoted by publishers and journals. You may find in here ideas for how you might transform the way you communicate with your students and vice versa. Do you have to be in the same room with your student to meet and discuss their practice skills? Is Skype or Adobe Connect an option or a language you just don't understand? There are several hosted debates on Twitter, as well as practitioner blogs and online discussion forums which seek to promote service user and carer perspectives. Put simply, as long as you have an internet connection there is a whole world of knowledge available to you and which you can direct your students towards. The authors of the chapters in this book illustrate in the activities they discuss that the use of social media brings educational benefits as well as social ones.

This book will also be a useful resource for social work academics particularly if you would like to engage with social media but fear the technological challenge, or are simply resistant to using technology in your teaching. Do you feel like other social work academics unhappy that students are using laptops, smart phones and tablets in your lectures? Would you feel like this if you knew that students were looking up references you had just presented, or the website of an organisation that supports service users? Or connecting on Twitter with the author of a research journal article you mentioned? Embracing social media involves reflecting on our own approaches to teaching and learning, recognising that a key part of our role is to encourage students to take responsibility for their own learning and there are a range of ways to access learning resources which enable them to reflect on their values and develop the knowledge and skills needed. Most of these ways will not involve spending hours in a library ploughing through volumes and photo-copying articles and book chapters. Did you spend your undergraduate years crawling around the floor of a library, standing at the photocopier collecting paper – highlighting documents you had printed to within an inch of their lives? It is perhaps timely that you capitalised on these technological innovations in your teaching and the authors in this text will illustrate how they have achieved just this, as trailblazers they also describe some of the challenges they experienced in doing so.

WHY IS SOCIAL MEDIA IMPORTANT FOR SOCIAL WORK EDUCATORS AND STUDENTS?

Globally there are 554,750,000 registered Twitter users, and on average 58 million tweets per day. There are 1.4 billion Facebook users (Statistics Brain, 2013); some of these will be social workers and social work students, and service users or carers. Increasingly there are forums for service users and carers. Although little is known about the development of online service user forums which use social media, there are concerns about the blurring of boundaries between social workers and how they communicate with service users. Ayres (2011a) and BASW (2012) Social Media Policy highlight this. Social media has been harnessed by campaigning organisations con-cerned with social issues which social workers deal with on a daily basis and which academics and social work researchers study. Social media is thus more than simply a connection device, it has an awareness raising angle which brings important social issues and the impact of social inequalities to the fore with immediacy and has been the promotion and communication arm of many recent welfare and social justice cam-paigns and challenges.

In a recent lecture with BA social work students we discussed how social media and/or online communication strategies might be utilised to support service users. The students listed several ideas that they thought would be useful ways of delivering services which included examples such as using Skype to virtually meet with service users who suffered from anxiety; encouraging service users to access online counselling services; providing benefit advice online; facilitating online discussion/support group for parents, or women who have experienced domestic violence. The students also suggested that using these strategies would be particularly useful in a rural context or others where social work per-sonnel may be stretched or unavailable. In a research project I was recently involved in the organisation communicates with their service users using a private Facebook group. The Facebook group is staffed for set hours every week so that the service users can contact the organisation and seek advice or support. The project worker also posts infor-mation about forthcoming events and real-time meetings on Facebook. This organisa-tion, which is in the voluntary sector, has a well-established social media policy and com-municates ordinarily with service users (all young people aged 9–24) via text.

As these examples suggest, and they are by no means unique, if organisations working with service users and carers are beginning to adopt online and specifically social media strategies not only to promote their work, but also as a way of delivering their services, it requires educators and students to develop an understanding of these methods, and to also be informed as to the potential difficulties or value issues which using social media presents.

Siemens (2005) charts the technological developments we have witnessed in the last few decades and identified trends in learning which suggest that as well as moving across and between learning environments, the way we learn and the places and contexts we learn in are likely to change. Technology changes the way in which we learn and how we access what we need to know, we use technology for some learning behaviours, and we use them differently throughout our lifetime. In the 1980s I could recite dozens of telephone numbers of friends and family, now I know two, the rest are stored on a SIM card as I don't need to keep them stored in my brain. Importantly Siemens suggests that the knowledge we need is specific as the locations of where this knowledge is has expanded, we need to know *where* to find out what we need to know. In higher education (HE) and in social work education and training the potential for information overload is vast, and this, coupled with the sheer amount of information which is available online suggests that we need to be selective, and critically informed about the resources we access and also about where we access these from.

Ayres on behalf of the HEA (2012) conducted a survey with social work academics exploring how they are using social media to support student learning. In the report Ayres argues that

> *Academics have an important role in ensuring that student social workers, like many professionals, have an appropriate online presence while remaining alive to the potential benefits of engaging though social media for practice educators, service users and carers.*

> (p 3)

There were 29 social work academics working in 19 UK universities and three US universities who participated in the survey and 80% of respondents were involved in both qualifying and post-qualifying social work education. The findings of the survey indicated that academics participating were keen to develop their knowledge and use of social media but needed support from their institutions to do this. There were several barriers to progressing with the inclusion of social media expressed by the respondents: having the necessary skills, and support from managers as well as fear of technology.

Respondents suggested that their university's use of social media could be developed by receiving training and information, case studies and good practice examples and regular updates on new developments. The majority (75%) of respondents provide training and support for their practice educators but very few communicated with practice educators using social media. This study's findings also suggested that training for academics, guidance, and information on developments and good practice were essential to develop the use of social media in social work education.

WHERE DID THE IDEAS FOR THIS BOOK COME FROM?

Some of us first met in Birmingham in April 2013 at an HEA funded *Changing the Learning Landscape* workshop. We were using social media to some degree in our teaching and learning, and studying, and keen to collaborate. This short video provides participant feedback about their experiences of a hands-on social media workshop run for the Changing the Learning Landscape Higher Education Academy series of events. Tarsem Singh Cooner and his colleague Chris Allen discuss the aims and outcomes for participants: www.youtube.com/watch?v=91P0eLzdGv0

In July 2013 all of the authors of this book met at the JSWEC conference at Royal Holloway, you can see the keynote lectures here:
www.bambuser.com/v/3730719

We were all delivering papers about our work using social media in our education. Liz Thackray has written about technological innovations on her profile on Academia.edu (www.independent.academia.edu/LizThackray). These and other hubs host information about work being undertaken and provide links to Twitter and Facebook for immediate global promotion. I have used Storify to capture and publicise research and teaching activities in promoting the digital activities of the School of Social Work (www.storify.com/jlwestwood/academic-networks). You can see here how Tarsem Singh Cooner uses a short YouTube film to introduce himself and the module to his students (www.youtube.com/watch?v=NK__XflZOG4). David McKendrick posts audio recordings of interviews with social work practitioners and academics as well as officials involved in regulating the profession. In this sound cloud interview David interviews Anna Fowlie the Chief Executive of the Scottish Social Care Council:
www.soundcloud.com/#glasgow-caledonian-uni/talking-social-work-gcus-david

Amanda Taylor has recruited film and media students to assist her in capturing and promoting the Social Work Book Group which she discusses in her chapter in this volume: www.storify.com/AMLTaylor66/the-use-of-book-clubs-in-social-work-education. You can see a blog version of Denise Turner's chapter outlined here where she discusses her early experiences of starting to engage with social media, and the trepidation she initially felt about this: www.socialworkatsussex.wordpress.com/category/social-work-research.

It was clear that during the face to face discussions and the conversations we had on social media at the conference and in the weeks following that we were all very keen to document, capture, and share the learning from our early projects.

CHAPTER OUTLINE

In Chapter 1 Liz Thackray discusses some of the barriers which prevent us from engaging with social media. Thackray became involved in developing and using technologies for

HE whilst she was undertaking PhD research. She participated in several social media forums which helped to address some of the isolation. This chapter introduces theories about users of technology in higher education and asks us to reflect on our use of social media. Thackray also discusses her own experience of participating in social media forums as a research student.

In 2013 Amanda Taylor, David McKendrick, and myself carried out a cross national survey of student social work use of social networking services (SNS). The survey required students to create a Twitter account and engage in a debate about registration with regulatory bodies (in this case HCPC and SSSC). We discuss the background to this project and the findings of the survey in Chapter 2. Students participating in the study illustrate a sophisticated knowledge of SNS and key ways in which they were using SNS, especially Twitter to support their learning and development. The challenges we faced, including a complete (albeit brief) shutdown of power are discussed here.

Tarsem Singh Cooner discusses how the popular SNS Facebook can be used to support critical thinking amongst social work students in Chapter 3. The closed Facebook group which he developed facilitated students with opportunities to communicate with each other and share their ideas. The carefully designed process used in this innovative teaching project received positive evaluations from students, promotes a high degree of student directed learning and flexibility which students require.

In Chapter 4 Amanda Taylor discusses how she established a social work book group (SWBG) which was initially for first year undergraduates. The book group now involves students, academic, authors, and practitioners exploring social work theories in fictional narratives. Social media has enriched this project by encouraging wider involvement in the SWBG discussions. The project is now a national programme with student social workers from across the United Kingdom reading and discussing social work theory, policy, communication skills, and developing their understanding of the complexity of the human conditions.

David McKendrick illustrates how blogging can complement student learning and assist the development of academic writing in Chapter 5. McKendrick illustrates the potential of blogging and uses examples to show how blogging captures opinions, views and experiences which can be shared globally and can provide informal access to academic and practitioner issues.

Denise Turner presents an autoethnographic account of becoming an 'expert' in social media and discusses how as a PhD student facilitating a regular online discussion reduced for her the isolation which is common for research students to experience. In Chapter 6 she describes her journey from resistance to acceptance of social media, exploring the underlying fear and anxiety that may be familiar to readers.

In the concluding chapter of this book, the themes and issues raised in Chapters 1 to 6 are discussed together with suggestions for taking the ideas discussed in this book forwards.

1   Obstacles to and engagement with social media

Liz Thackray

INTRODUCTION

In this chapter, I present some theoretical models exploring the adoption of new ideas and technologies, and apply these models to the adoption of social media. I go on to explore some obstacles to engaging with social media and other technology, making some tentative suggestions as to how those resistant to embracing these technologies might be encouraged to engage with them. Throughout I draw on my own experience gained through involvement in the use of a range of social media, in particular Twitter based networks supporting postgraduate researchers.

Social media is a relatively new phenomenon. Ten years ago Twitter, Facebook, YouTube, Pinterest, Flickr!, LinkedIn, and other social media applications were at best a twinkle in somebody's eye. Words like 'app' had not entered our vocabulary. Mobile phones were no longer 'bricks', but had not yet become 'smart'. As social media applications began to emerge, interest grew in how social media might support practice based learning (Thackray et al., 2007; Scantlebury, 2008; Dunworth and Scantlebury, 2006; Scantlebury et al., 2008; Waldman and Rafferty, 2008). Recent years have seen a huge growth in what is sometimes described as Web 2.0 (DiNucci, 1999), as the World Wide Web has developed from static websites, equivalent to printed material that cannot be changed or commented on. Examples such as the home pages of most university websites may be likened to a printed prospectus, to dynamic websites that can be updated more easily. These do not usually include facilities for users to edit the content although there may be a facility to comment on content of many commercial and news websites. On social media sites the content is generated by users and can be commented on, as with blogs and photo sharing sites, or edited, as with wikis, the best known of which is Wikipedia©. This evolution has been enabled and accompanied by changes in technology leading to faster computers and operating systems, higher resolution imagery, and faster Internet access. Developments in wifi and mobile technologies and decreasing costs of Internet access has led to engagement with others through the Internet becoming increasingly ubiquitous. Despite Facebook, Twitter, 'friending' and 'tweeting' becoming part of everyday speech and words like 'selfie' being included in major dictionaries, there are variations in the extent to which social media has been embraced. Understandably some students and academics remain sceptical of the value of using social media platforms in learning contexts. This chapter explores the range of responses to social media. There are three key learning aims:

- You will be introduced to some of the technical language used by technologists, social scientists and others in discussing the adoption of social media and other technological developments.
- You will be introduced to different ideas about when and why people adopt new technologies and asked to reflect on how these models might extend beyond technology to other areas of life.
- You will consider some of the obstacles and challenges confronted by people in adopting new technologies.

Although much of the content of this chapter is theoretical, you are encouraged to consider your own response to innovation and change both in regard to social media and more generally.

ADOPTION OF NEW TECHNOLOGY

There is a distinction between those technology users termed 'digital natives', who have grown up with technology, and 'digital immigrants', who have only encountered computer technologies in adulthood (Prensky 2001). Prensky went on to suggest that this difference affected not only how younger people related to technology, but was reflected in how they learned. Despite Prensky's ideas being challenged by White and Le Cornu (2011) and others, the digital native/digital immigrant metaphor continues to be prevalent in discussions relating to the use of technology in learning contexts, resulting in a tendency to assume that students, especially younger ones, are familiar with computer technologies, including social media, and ready to embrace their possibilities. White and Le Cornu suggest instead that people are 'digital residents' or 'digital visitors' (2011) recognising that people vary in their level of comfort and familiarity with technology, independent of their age, gender, social background and education. The recognition that people vary in their response to new technologies is not new. As long ago as 1962, Rogers developed a model of the 'diffusion of innovation' that differentiated innovators (those who create new ideas and technologies) and early adopters (the first to acquire new shiny toys) from mainstream adopters of technology and those who only engage with a technology because they are required to by others. Moore (1991) extended this thinking to suggest there was a 'chasm' between early adopters and those that followed, stemming from differences in the attitudes and personalities of the two groups. This divide is reflected in the differentiation of 'digital natives and immigrants' and 'digital residents and visitors'.

Whereas these models view the adoption of technologies from the perspective of user differences, the US consultancy company, Gartner, focused on the life-cycle of technologies, in developing a model referred to as the 'hype cycle'. This model suggests that as a new technology is implemented by early adopters, interest is generated through the news media and discussion leading to a 'peak of inflated expectations' as to what this new technology might achieve. As others explore the technology, they find it does not meet their expectations, resulting in a 'trough of disillusionment' as the limitations of the technology become evident. Some innovations never move beyond this point. Others are adopted as their potential becomes more broadly understood and reasonable expectations for the technology are established. During the middle part of the first decade of the current century, there was a lot of excitement about the development of 3D virtual worlds, primarily Second Life. Some proponents viewed this as a Web 3.0 that would replace the Internet as we knew it and envisaged virtual university campuses and lecture theatres replacing physical buildings. Although the technology is still there it has become a niche interest with a few innovators continuing to develop some applications, but it is no longer viewed, at least for the present, as the next big thing. Other innovations have disappeared or been replaced.

The Diffusion of Innovations model (Rogers, 2003 [1962]; Moore, 1991; Geoghegan, 1994) and the Gartner Hype Cycle suggest that any technological innovation goes through a number of stages before it is accepted as a mainstream technology. They both identify a point when an innovation may be recognised and adopted by the mainstream of potential users, when it ceases to be of interest, or when it may be adopted and developed within a niche market. In both cases, it is recognised that initially a new technological development tends to be adopted and promoted by innovators, who develop the technology, followed by early adopters, who embrace the technology and publicise its affordances, sometimes raising unrealistic expectations. The Gartner Hype Cycle suggests that the end of this first stage of the adoption of a new technology is marked by a 'peak of inflated expectations', whereas the diffusion of innovations model suggests that the adoption of technology follows a bell-curve as mainstream users begin to adopt the technology, but there is a 'chasm' (Moore, 1991) that has to be crossed before mainstream users begin to adopt the technology. In 'crossing the chasm' or navigating the 'trough of disillusionment' a technology may cease to be of interest and effectively disappear, or users may establish realistic expectations of the affordances of the technology so that it continues to enter into mainstream usage.

Critical reflection

Take a few minutes to reflect on your own use of technology. Do you regard yourself as comfortable using technology or do you approach the unfamiliar with trepidation? Are you one of the first to upgrade your computer operating system or do you wait for the bugs to be found and fixed? Do you get the latest phone at the first opportunity, or do you continue to use the phone you got five years ago?

EASE OF USE AND ENGAGEMENT

Davis (1989) suggests that the relationship between 'perceived ease of use' of a new technology and its 'perceived usefulness' is fundamental for technology users in deciding whether or not to engage with it. During the first decade of the current century there was considerable interest in 3D virtual worlds within a wide range of disciplines from social care and counselling to molecular sciences to literature to psychology to computer sciences. A number of universities and other institutions invested large sums of money in developing simulations and using these virtual environments in a variety of different ways. A series of surveys (Kirriemuir, 2007; Kirriemuir, 2008; Kirriemuir, 2009b; Kirriemuir, 2009a) found an increasing engagement in virtual worlds by universities to the point where only two UK higher education institutions did not have a presence in Second Life™, a popular online world. However, a major stumbling block was engaging both teachers and students in using the technology in order for it to become mainstream. It was clear the technology offered something interesting and potentially useful. Coventry University developed a virtual care home and Imperial College a virtual hospital, both of which were used with students and in continuing professional development. However, the learning curve necessary to access the technology and use it effectively was very steep, even for computer scientists (Thackray et al., 2010) and universities and funding bodies have withdrawn from investigating these technologies further. Although the potential usefulness of the technology was evident, the learning curve was too steep to encourage mainstream adoption and usage.

Moore (1991) not only suggested that there was a 'chasm' between early adopters of a new technology and those users forming the 'early majority' of mainstream users, but that there were more fundamental differences between the individuals comprising these groups. Whereas early adopters are interested in the technology itself, are visionary in respect of its potential and welcome change, being prepared to take risks and solve technical problems, mainstream users tend to be both more pragmatic and risk averse, needing to know that an application will work and be useful to them and that support is available should it be required. If an application is difficult to use and its perceived usefulness is limited, it is unlikely to be attractive to mainstream users.

Critical reflection

Take a few minutes to reflect on your own use of technology and social media. Think about a software application or 'gadget' you have used in the past, but no longer use. What attracted you to the technology? Why did you stop using it?

Social media is ubiquitous; applications such as Twitter™, Facebook™, and YouTube™ are household names. However educators and students vary in the extent to which they embrace these technologies in an educational context. The uptake of technology is of interest in considering the use of social media in social work education, and in higher education more generally. What is it that leads to some technologies being adopted in educational settings and others dropping off the radar? The remainder of this chapter draws on the experience of developing Twitter based support networks to explore some of the obstacles that lead to resisting the adoption of new technologies and makes some suggestions as to how these might be addressed.

OBSTACLES TO ENGAGING WITH TECHNOLOGY

Ever since Prensky (2001) suggested younger technology users were essentially different from older ones, using the metaphor of digital natives and immigrants, there has been a tendency to assume that younger people are competent users of technology unlike their elders and teachers. However in a review of student use of technology, Thorpe and Edmunds came to the conclusion that '*incoming cohorts of undergraduates are not homogenous with regard to their use of Web 2.0 tools and approaches and their ICT skills generally*' (2011: 386). If this is the case, it is probable that social work students, representing a wider age range than traditional undergraduates, are likely to vary even more in their familiarity with technology. Drawing on the findings of White and Le Cornu (2011), age is not a good indicator of digital literacy, but rather 'digital residents' are comfortable with technology, familiar with different platforms and applications and have developed ways of approaching unfamiliar technologies and gaining support in using them, while 'digital visitors' recognise the need for a passing acquaintance with a variety of applications, but have little interest in the technology per se. As the use of web-based tools, repositories and environments has been shown to be useful in social work training (Waldman and Rafferty, 2008), workplace learning, continuing professional development (Billett, 2008) and providing access to evidence-based practice (Gilgun, 2005), it is relevant to explore further the obstacles that lead some people to reject some technologies.

In studies of introducing learners to Second Life™ Warburton (2008; 2009) and Thackray et al. (2008; 2010) identify a number of obstacles that need to be overcome before learners are willing to engage with the technology. These obstacles are considered here in relation to introducing social media to social work and other students in higher education settings.

TECHNICAL ISSUES

Students may be unsure how to use an unfamiliar application, may have concerns about the security of the technology, and may need to know more about persistence and the durability of material placed on Web 2.0 platforms. Whereas it is relatively straightforward to provide support in accessing an application through written instructions and mentoring, some students find learning to use a new application technically challenging and some need a positive incentive to persuade them to engage with it at all. It is not uncommon to hear potential users speak of the complexity of Twitter, perhaps in terms of 'just not getting it'. Concerns about security and durability can be complex and do have a basis in reality. Students may be concerned that the use of some technologies may facilitate others accessing and misusing their account (hacking). They may worry about the risk of infection by a virus, Trojan, or other 'nasty' making it impossible to use their computer. It is possible to include digital literacy within the curriculum and to offer guidance on good computing practice. Most universities have a code of practice and many employers also offer support, advice and guidance in developing good digital practices. Institutions may provide students with anti-virus and other protective software for use on their own equipment. However it is not possible to guarantee that any computer usage is risk-free. For some risk averse, non-tech-savvy students, the risks may be too great to countenance, especially when using personal equipment, also used by other family members, rather than institution or employer provided and supported equipment. Although using social media is no more risky than using email or an Internet search engine, for some users the perception is interacting with others in real time on social media sites is inevitably more risky. This perception is often reinforced by anecdotal accounts of problems encountered by friends or colleagues.

Concerns about the durability of digital material are realistic. It is common to warn young people to be careful what they write on their Facebook™ pages as these may be viewed by potential employers or university admissions tutors. Recent news stories include accounts of prosecutions for posting inappropriate comments on social media sites. In 2013, a young person appointed as a police youth commissioner in Kent resigned her post when her inappropriate Twitter comments were made public. Even innocuous material can have a long digital life; an Internet search on my name reveals contributions I made to a student forum in 1999. Although I personally do not find it problematic to have this digital footprint, others may be less sanguine about such material continuing to be accessible in the public domain.

IDENTITY

Each of us has many different identities reflecting the many relationships and roles we occupy. In the case of social work students, engaging in the use of social media implies the development of a professional persona in an online space – and a space where the individual may already have a personal persona. Some students use social media applications within their friendship network, but may hesitate to use the same applications in a learning or professional context. Having a public persona has implications for relationships with colleagues, managers, teachers and service users. Whereas the role and relationship between teacher and student are clearly understood in most educational and professional settings, there may be a need to renegotiate those relationships in social media settings (Savin-Baden et al., 2008). Online communications differ from those in classrooms and other structured settings; they are not constricted in time and space. Teachers may find students expect more interaction online than in physical spaces (Thackray et al., 2010). Tensions may arise between professional communications and the playfulness or informality of interactions in a more social and less formal environment (Warburton, 2009). Questions arise as to whether students and teachers are happy to 'follow' or 'friend' each other. Further, is it acceptable to 'friend' or be followed by a service user? This issue is explored further by Tarsem Singh Cooner who developed the *Social Work Social Media App* (see Chapter 3 of this volume).

Critical reflection

Consider your Facebook account for a moment. Would you be happy for your tutor to see it? Or a service user? How would you respond to a friend request from a young person you are working with?

VISIBILITY PRIVACY AND CONFIDENCE

Being visible online can carry risks. Publishing photos of partners and offspring presents a different persona to service users and others than the more sanitised professional persona. Some may worry about possible undesirable consequences of such visibility and the potential for placing others at risk. Ask yourself, do I want images of my child or my partner to be accessible to service users? Do I want them to receive 'friending' requests from people I encounter through my work? One way of addressing this is choosing to have more than one online identity, separating personal and professional lives. Once an online presence is established, it is impossible to maintain privacy completely, even when using settings incorporated in the application that assist protection of privacy. As such social work students, professionals, and academics must always bear in mind that privacy is limited.

Even confident social media users can experience difficulties with online communication. Feeling 'at home' with technology can lead some people to use the technology as a place to express negative feelings, complain about those they work with, and write things that might be expressed to close friends in a private conversation, but do not belong in a public space. Such behaviours may at best affect how a person is perceived, but carry the risk of committing an illegal act which can lead to criminal charges or civil action, as in libel proceedings initiated by Lord McAlpine and the jailing of the abusers of Caroline Criado Perez following inappropriate use of Twitter.

There is a growing tendency to live 'life on the screen' (Turkle, 1996). Such online living is changing the ways in which we interact with and relate to each other socially (Turkle, 2004; 2011; Baym, 2010). Although many of these changes are positive, Turkle (2011) suggests even technology enthusiasts should take a more nuanced perspective on how online living affects our non-digital encounters. As an aside, Turkle's accounts of the care of elderly and vulnerable people being entrusted to robots should perhaps be required reading for all with an interest in social welfare and social policy.

CULTURE, COLLABORATION, AND COST

All communities are based on codes of practice and rules of etiquette, even though these may not be formalised. When we move to a new locality, we may find neighbourhood expectations that determine how we relate to neighbours and local tradespeople and these expectations may differ from where we lived previously. Similarly, social media has its own rules and expectations. Some of these may be generalised, as in what has become known as 'netiquette', while others are specific to the social media platform. Such rules govern the way in which users contribute to the life of the community and communicate with each other. They relate to the format of messages, the posting of photos, tweets, links, etc. and the ways in which users respond to each other. Failure to meet cultural expectations can result in a loss of followers and being 'unfriended'. Inappropriate promotion of others contributions can be problematic, as when retweeting without acknowledging the original author. As in the non-digital world, many of the unwritten rules are learned by osmosis through engagement with others.

Critical reflection

Think about your use of social media. What rules are you aware of?

The underlying purpose for engaging in online communities and using social media is the development of personal, professional and social networks (Lewis and Rush, 2013). Community building requires participation, but what forms of participation are necessary and appropriate online? Hrastinski (2008) identified six levels of participation by learners with online media, ranging from simply accessing the environment to reading, writing and participating in dialogue. Although content and communication is necessary for a community to grow and develop, it is too simplistic to equate participation in a community only with the production and posting of content. Consideration also needs to be given to the contribution made by those who mainly engage by reading the contributions of others. Although such users may be denigrated as 'lurkers' or 'passive recipients' (Romiszowski and Mason as cited in Hrastinski, 2008,p 1760), such activity may actually indicate active reflection and engagement in learning. Wenger (1998) suggests that participation in a community of practice is a combination of doing, talking, thinking, feeling and belonging. Thus it is possible to 'participate socially even at times when we are not engaged in a conversation with someone' (Hrastinski, 2008,p. 1760). The first step to engagement with social media, as with non-digital interaction, can be lurking and becoming familiar with the new environment.

Most social media and Web 2.0 applications do not involve financial costs beyond those associated with accessing an Internet enabled digital device. However there can be other costs for social work students, who are often very busy people, balancing home, work, and study commitments and attempting to maintain some personal space. Engaging with social media can be time intensive and may lead some to question whether it is worth making the necessary investment of time in order to engage effectively online. If the learning curve is too steep, or the perceived usefulness of the technology is too little, there may be a resistance to making any engagement with the technology (Davis, 1989; Thorpe and Gordon, 2012).

ENGAGING WITH SOCIAL MEDIA – REFLECTING ON #PHDCHAT

Towards the end of 2010, whilst I was a research student I was made aware of a number of other postgraduate researchers who were communicating on Twitter using the hashtag #phdchat. At the time, I had had a Twitter account for several months, but I was a Twitter user; I had not found a way of engaging with the medium and I did not consider it a valuable resource. However a colleague encouraged me to look at #phdchat, and I logged in on a Wednesday evening to a moderated discussion. Although I am an experienced computer user and have been involved in online learning and teaching for several years, I could not envisage an in-depth academic conversation taking place on Twitter. I found myself engaging in a lively discussion with a small group of postgraduate researchers from different disciplines and at different stages in their doctoral journeys. Although being restricted to 140 characters was a challenge, the discussion was both interesting and relevant. It was as though I had stumbled across an online common room where it was possible to share concerns, ask questions and offer encouragement and support to others. Over the course of the next few days, I discovered #phdchat did not only exist in the Wednesday evening space, but, by using the hashtag, I was able to find and communicate with other research students at virtually any time of day or night. News of #phdchat spread rapidly – perhaps it was filling a gap felt by many lonely researchers – and by early 2011, two months after the first moderated chat, over one hundred different individuals from all over the globe had participated in the weekly chat sessions by tweeting or retweeting and others had read the conversations. Individual participants had established a Facebook group, a diigo list (for sharing links to useful articles and books) and a wiki (where an archive of chats was established and where members of the #phdchat community developed shared resources). Three years on, #phdchat is a thriving community that continues to meet on Wednesday evenings and to offer support during the week. Personally, I found the support of colleagues engaging in #phdchat invaluable in enabling me to complete my PhD.

What has made this initiative so effective in drawing together research students and developing a community of practice?

The first observation is the commitment and enthusiasm of the early adopters. Once a time had been established for the weekly chat sessions, one member of the group undertook the task of posting a weekly 'tweet' publicising the topic that would be discussed the following week. Others 'retweeted' the notice, ensuring the chat sessions were publicised. The discussion topics were determined by participants who voted in a weekly poll and suggested other topics for discussion. A wiki was established where chats were archived. Participants in the chats encouraged each other by setting challenges, for example writing a blog post describing their research in plain English. The list of research topics and the URLs for the blog posts was added to the wiki. These actions created a sense of community and working together and could be seen as the beginnings of an emerging community of practice.

Second, participants in #phdchat took the opportunity to publicise the initiative. A number of people wrote blog posts. Some included mention of #phdchat in presentations given to colleagues. This was not just advertising a new product, but #phdchatters were sharing ways in which they had gained from engagement with the #phdchat community. As well as being a new initiative, it was well worth exploring because of what it had to offer.

Third, #phdchat was developing a presence on Twitter. By using the hashtag, it was possible to engage with other research students. Not infrequently a question would be asked about a methodology or where to find a particular reference and an answer would quickly appear. As the 'tweets' were visible to anybody searching the hashtag, it soon became clear that this was a valuable and knowledgeable resource. In addition, the fact that other postgraduate researchers were online meant that the #phdchat community could be used as a support group. It was possible to send a tweet on a Saturday morning asking who else was working, to receive five or six responses and to arrange to take a virtual coffee break with those individuals later in the morning.

It is unclear what the critical mass of membership is that is necessary for an online community to be successful, but #phdchat quickly established a membership that was large enough to ensure a lively discussion each Wednesday. Even though the same people moderated and archived the chat for the first two years of the life of #phdchat, as they progressed towards the end of their doctoral journeys, it became clear that the community had to take ownership of its own continuity. The wiki was used to establish a hosting rota and various participants offered to take responsibility for Wednesday chat sessions, sometimes suggesting the discussion topic and sometimes using a poll to engage others. Initially, this was a difficult time for #phdchat but there was a sense of the community being too important to allow its demise and it is now even more firmly established and owned by those who use it and have made an investment in the community. The experience of participants in #phdchat is not unusual. Lewis and Rush (2013) have explored the development of networks and communities of practice in Twitter and other chapters in this volume describe other experiences of using social media in a variety of ways.

CONCLUSIONS

Introducing a new technology to students in any discipline presents a number of challenges and obstacles. For social work students, it is essential to protect a professional identity and set boundaries while at the same time learning what are deemed as acceptable risks. Even though a technology may look interesting, and may appear useful, unless it is perceived as accessible, easy to use, and presenting clear benefits, it is unlikely to be adopted unless there is an incentive to do so. The best advocates for any technology, including social media are those who are not only enthusiastic users of the technology, but those who are able to share their own stories of how they have gained from using the technology.

2 Student social workers use of social media: findings from a cross-national survey

Joanne Westwood, Amanda Taylor, and David McKendrick

INTRODUCTION

This chapter discusses the development and implementation of a project to engage BA undergraduate social work students in a Twitter debate the topic of which was the merits of registration with a regulatory body. Currently English social work students are not required to register with the regulatory body, the Health Care Professions Council (HCPC), but Scottish students are required to register with the Scottish Social Care Council (SSSC) and to comply with the respective codes of conduct. Our aims in this research were to encourage social work students to use Twitter to complement their classroom learning, to participate in a Twitter debate about registration with a regulatory body and complete an online pre and post-debate survey. The project was designed to support them to set up a Twitter account and interact with other social work students. The project was based in two sites, one in England and one in Scotland and involved 50 students and 3 social work educators. The different registration requirements for both sets of students formed the basis of the discussion during the debate. This chapter provides a background discussion about Twitter and how this led to the development and implementation of this study. We then discuss the findings of the survey questionnaire which captures the views of social work students in regards to their use of social media.

BACKGROUND

There are a range of social networking services (SNS) which can be used to support student learning in and beyond the traditional classroom. Twitter is an SNS which was launched in 2006. It has grown into a global social media service and it is on Twitter where news about important national and international events are first made public. Twitter users are called tweeps, and they post tweets onto their Twitter account. Tweeps have followers who can read the tweets, reply, or re-tweet (circulate to their own followers). Tweeting is restricted to a maximum of 140 characters which limits the length and detail of tweets and means that tweeps have to be succinct to get their message across. Twitter is a forum where celebrities share their habits, interests, and opinions and more recently has grown popular with academics for teaching, research, and networking (Lewis and Rush 2013).The deaths of Nelson Mandela, the criminologist Jock Young, the sociologist Stan Cohen, and the cultural theorist Stuart Hall were all reported on Twitter simultaneously with official television news media broadcasts. The authors of this chapter, all former practitioners and social work academics, are keen tweeps and have all experienced several benefits of using Twitter in their teaching and research. Twitter has also been used by the authors to connect with the UK social work academic and practice communities as well as internationally, and, to a lesser extent with service users and carers.

The initial idea for the project developed as a discussion on Twitter between the three authors. Making the project a reality involved us having a dialogue which was conducted online using various platforms including Skype, Adobe Connect, and direct messaging on Twitter as well as good old fashioned email. Our combined experience of Twitter at this stage was limited to joining in debates and discussions from time to time, following and networking with other social work academics and organisations. We all agreed that the debates were useful learning opportunities for students to engage in and we were keen to understand how we could facilitate that engagement. We were concerned that student's use of social media in their education was problematised in terms of their being disruptive, and there did not appear to be an acceptance that encouraging the use of social media in the learning space might be facilitating learning and development. We were keen to identify how as educators we might capitalise on students' eagerness for and adeptness in their use of social media and alert them to how this might be channelled into using social media to support their skills, knowledge and values development. As we developed the ideas for the debate it became apparent that we knew little about our own students' engagement with social media and social networking for learning and so we devised a short survey to capture this information. We also wanted to gain some understanding of how students engaged with the debate we were hosting and to what extent their experiences of the debate would influence their continued use of social media and specifically social networking sites for their learning.

SOCIAL WORK REGULATORY BODIES AND SOCIAL MEDIA

Alongside the growth more broadly of social media services and social networking sites such as Twitter, codes of conduct have been developed in response to concerns about professional boundaries, and accessibility of personal information posted on Twitter by both service users and social workers. It is thus a real issue in social work practice which those involved in education and training of social work students must embrace. Schrembi (2008) wrote about the potential of new technologies for social worker educators and practitioners illustrating several different ways in which they could support service user empowerment, and how social workers were ideally placed to advise policy makers about online safety issues. Duncan Daston et al. (2013) in the US context discuss the ethical issues related to social media and social work education. They draw our attention to the priority which social work educators must give to ensuring that their students are informed about the professional codes of conduct which apply. Social media services such as Twitter whilst virtual are also utilised by students to communicate and share personal information. The professional codes of conduct which apply in the four nations of the UK are in place to ensure that students are accountable for their professional conduct and boundaries in all form of communication including social networking platforms such as Twitter.

The College of Social Work (2013) in its 'Process curriculum: Enhancing the professional nature of social work education' document instructs that, 'programmes will use a range of approaches to teaching and learning using both didactic and interactive methods. Some will be delivered face to face, some through e-learning or a combination (blended learning)'; more significantly it advises that, 'in order to fully engage with their course, students will need to understand the rationale for these varied approaches to learning and how they support the development of the qualities and skills expected of social workers' (p. 3). Therefore, if social work practice is to be deemed contemporary the delivery methods employed in social work education will require academics to have a comprehensive understanding of the various digital platforms available and more particularly those which are accessible to both the student and more importantly the service-user. Given that we know students are coming into Higher Education institutions with a variety of social media skills we considered it was important to gauge their level of expertise and use of social media through the survey.

Since May 2004 social work students in Scotland are required to be registered with the national governing body the Scottish Social Services Council, the same arrangements are in place with the other Celtic nations ie Wales, and Northern Ireland. Exploring the perceptions of students on this issue was of interest to us as researchers as we were aware of the cross national anomaly created by the decision of the HCPC not to register students and the registration of students in the rest of the United Kingdom. Equally we were not aware of any research into students' attitudes to this particular cross national difference in approach. We were aware of a body of work that related to registration and the particular functions it has including Wiles (2009) Orme and Rennie (2006). The purpose of registration being summarised as:

- to protect service users and the public;
- to raise the status of the profession;
- to control the workforce.

The first of these functions represent the role and task of social workers throughout the world. The protection of the vulnerable and the protection of wider society are central tenets of social work activity and are enshrined in a variety of legislative instruments. The second aspect was of greater interest to us as researchers; registration is seen as part of promoting the notion of professionalism suggesting that prior to registration being implemented social work was not seen as professional and needed support to be elevated to professional status (Orme and Rennie, 2009). Interestingly however registration is not equated in any of the registering bodies with broader themes of social justice or supporting political change; registration relates to a particular area of social work activity framed around the powerful notion of 'protection'.

Critical reflection

Are there any current issues in social work which might be useful for engaging students in an online debate?

TECHNOLOGY AND ITS PLACE IN CONTEMPORARY SOCIAL WORK EDUCATION

If contemporary social work practice demands contemporary social work practitioners then social work education must have a contemporary ethos. The regulating bodies' that inform social work education attend to quality and monitor the robustness of the curricula. They stipulate requirements that promote contemporary approaches but lack depth, in terms of the development of the knowledge base in relation to the use of technology from either the service-user or practitioner perspectives. Included in professional guidance is reference to the safety, risk, and professionalism agendas but generally these are less progressive from an educational position This signifies the need for a more explicit, current, and proactive response to this area of the skills base in terms of social media and use of learning technologies broadly if we are to continue with the claim that social work is unquestionably 'contemporary' in its approach.

Notably literature citing the case for and outlining the beginnings of a knowledge base for technology in contemporary social work education and practice remains oddly in its infancy even though it was being discussed and promoted in the most futuristic terms as far back as the early 1990s see (Rafferty, 1997) for a thorough and grounding account; one that the raises questions about the disparate nature of the relationship between social work and technology. Historically, but not surprisingly, social work creativity has been suppressed by a lack of funding, risk adverse policies and government directives that are often short-sighted and reactionary. It is imperative that social work as a profession states 'its' way forward in an attempt to be more 'responsive' and less 'reactive' to risk. Given that the present-day landscape of risk is, often, associated with technology via social networking and social media, further thought and additional attention is needed with regards to the potential hazards that each pose for the practitioners, service-users and carers. We make the case that the problematic nature of issues that can arise through online activity dictates that there is more than just the maintaining of professionalism at stake here; and that facilitating learning about these issues lies firmly at the door of social work education.

Critical reflection

What technological innovations do you use in your teaching and/or practice which have led you to consider and reflect on your professional value base?

METHODS

Ethical approval for this study was granted by the University of Central Lancashire ethics committee and Glasgow Caledonian University ethics committee. We encouraged students in both locations to consider their conduct in light of the expectations of the Universities and in the case of the Scottish students in light of their position as registered social work students. First year undergraduate student social workers were recruited into the study and participated in the online Twitter debate as part of communication and interpersonal skills modules which are delivered in both institutions. All participants were invited to join a private Twitter site for the debate, and were provided with detailed instructions on how to set up a Twitter account. Prior to the study starting all participants provided written consent.

THE SURVEY

Before the debate began participants were invited to complete an online survey which asked questions about their engagement with social networking services (SNS).

Pre debate survey questions:

- Would you say your use of SNS has changed since you started university?
- Which SNS would you say you use for supplementing your studies? (tick all that apply)
- During self-directed study time do you engage with any of the following?
- Which online environment has been most effective in supplementing your learning?
- How has your use of SNS developed your communication skills?
- When learning outside the class room/seminar group could you rate the quality of this experience?
- Which SNS would you recommend to your peers?

Once participants had completed the survey the debate began. A member of the research team based at UCLan posted the debate questions onto the private Twitter account. Questions were focussed around the topic of student registration with a regulatory body, and about their developing professional value base. Students responded with comments and questions using a 'hashtag' (#) which enabled us to capture and archive their contributions as date for analysis. In total there were five questions as follows:

1: Do you think that social work students should register with a relevant governing body? In Scotland this is required but not in England.
2: What do you see as the potential benefits/restrictions of registration? List.
3: In what ways do you think registration could contribute to changes in your online behaviour?
4: How do you think social work students could protect their online social profile?
5: What would you do if you noticed another social worker behaving in a manner that did not uphold public trust and represent the profession in a manner that is in keeping with HCPC/SSSC Standards?

Once the debate was finished participants were invited to complete a post survey online questionnaire which was designed to determine to what extent being involved in the debate influenced their future use of SNS and their online presence/profile.

- How would you rate your experience of the Twitter debate?
- Has participating in the Twitter debate made you think about your changing your online profile?

- Are there any SNS you might use as a result of participating in this debate?
- Are there any barriers to your using SNS?
- Which environment has been most effective in supporting your learning?
- Has participating in the Twitter debate had any impact on your communication skills?
- Will you use SNS to communicate with service users?
- Will you use SNS to communicate with other students or social work academic/practitioners?

The Twitter debate was archived for later analysis. The survey responses were thematically analysed and are discussed below.

FINDINGS

Pre-survey responses

In terms of the pre survey there were some interesting findings. In responding to the question about the change in using social media since starting university 90% of the 50 participants who completed the survey agreed that this had changed. The students who commented on the change reported that using Twitter had increased their professionalism and had led to contact with social workers from other parts of the world:

> *I only ever used Facebook before starting Uni, I now use Twitter to communicate with other social workers from all over the world, and I find it very interesting to see how different people view things.*

In responding to the question about which SNS they use, students reported use of multiple SNS (see Table 2.1 which illustrates the range). The percentages do not add up to 100% as students were able to indicate as many different SNS as they used.

As illustrated in Table 2.1, Twitter, YouTube, Skype, and Facebook were the most popular SNS used which suggests a pattern of engagement and new forms of student directed research which leads from the use of one SNS to the use of another. One of the research team uses ADOBE Connect/Skype regularly to communicate with students and the use of these may be related to this exposure.

The next question in the pre-debate survey asked about use of SNS during self-directed study time:

Again multiple platforms are used by students to support their learning and development. Whilst not all of these SNS are strictly social media platforms (Turnitin for example) the majority do offer the opportunity for online or real time interaction. These findings also demonstrate that the majority of students are engaging with SNS to complement their learning and knowledge acquisition when they are outside of the traditional classroom.

Table 2.1 *To show use of named SNS*

Facebook	34%
Twitter	94%
Linkedin	6%
Skype	38%
Instagram	2%
YouTube	60%
MSN messenger	6%
Adobe Connect	12%
imessage, kick	6%
BBM messenger	2%
Facetime	8%

Table 2.2 *To show which SNS students use in self-directed study time*

E skills	60%	30
Twitter	84%	42
Discussion board	72%	36
ICT based learning activities (Blackboard)	56%	28
SCIE TV	8%	4
GCULearn,	10%	5
TURNITIN	64%	32
IRISS	10%	5
The cloud	10%	5
YouTube	70%	35

Not surprising the online environment most effective in supplementing student learning was the official institutions VLE. However the responses to this question which asked students to state which SNS they use illustrated that 84% were also using Twitter. These responses suggest that students are using Twitter to network locally and globally: '*Twitter has enabled me to keep up to date with current issues within social work and keeps me in touch with other academics and agencies*' and are able to discriminate between what is relevant both now and in the future: '*On Twitter I read a range of different stories, which often may not be relatable to current parts of my course, but are of benefit to me to read and will be useful for future purposes.*' The ability to network with professionals and across year groups was also welcomed and highlighted the importance of informal peer mentoring and exchanges between students on different cohorts: '*Twitter as I can speak to other professionals and students including 2nd and 3rd years who prove great support.*' One of the research team had instituted the practice of sending revision prompts, advice and links on Twitter and this had been well received by student followers who were preparing for an examination: '*Twitter – good revision prompts.*'

On the whole students reported that SNS developed their communication skills in several key ways: For some students it had enabled them to build a professional profile and supported the development of their professional identity. Other students reported a growing self-awareness and confidence to be proactive in their efforts at communication and building relationships with other professionals, extending and developing their professional and social networks. For other students being able to access relevant materials speedily had helped them, which suggests that strategies of disseminating teaching and /or research materials on Twitter which is relevant to student learning, is taken up and used to supplement traditional classroom based learning. Twitter is perceived as a valuable source of research materials and has helped in developing an understanding of academic language and the appropriate use of language in their communication.

There is evidence that students are discerning in their use of SNS as highlighted in the response '*Twitter for the social work course, I use Facebook for more personal and friends.*' In addition this student statement suggests that using Twitter promoted them to reflect on what they were saying in their tweets because it was going to be available on a public forum '*I think about what I am going to write before I do because I know everyone is going to read it*', and again, the interpretation of tweet posts was explained here: '*I now think more carefully about what I type before tweeting or posting as the way things are read often come across differently.*' These responses suggest that student social workers in this study have developed sensitivity to the implications of their Twitter contributions and posts.

There were responses from several students which suggested that they do not think that using Twitter has contributed towards the development of their communication skills, in this case the student report that: '*It hasn't developed my communication skills as I am rarely on it but when I am on it my communication skills do not develop but degrade for some reason. Maybe because my grammar is not as good.*' Here we see reference to the 140 character limits of Twitter posts and the difficulty in expressing a view or opinion within this. The ability to write succinctly and correctly can be somewhat compromised when we are forced to squeeze our thought into this rigid character requirement.

Post-debate survey

We received 46 responses to this survey. About 96% (43) participants agreed that they had enjoyed the debate, one participant did not and two other participants reported that *it was a good experience but a bit rushed* and *a bit difficult to follow*.

Nearly 30% of participants agreed that participating in the debate had made them think about changing their online profile, and two thirds of responses indicated that they would not implement any changes. Participants were invited to qualify their responses further and many reported that they had made changes when they became a student social worker and recognised the potential risks. For participants from Scotland this had been prompted when they registered with SSSC and for these in England induction onto the course had included discussion of online conduct. Of the participants who believed they did not need to make any changes, they stated that they had made sufficient changes to

Table 2.3 *Are there any social networking services you might use as a result of participating in this debate?*

Answer Options	Response Percent	Response Count
E skills	43.5%	20
Twitter	89.1%	41
Discussion board	52.2%	24
ICT based learning activities (Blackboard)	32.6%	15
SCIE TV	0.0%	0
GCULearn,	4.3%	2
TURNITIN	37.0%	17
Slideshare	0.0%	0
SWAPbox	2.2%	1
IRISS	4.3%	2
The cloud	10.9%	5
You tube	43.5%	20
Other (please specify)		4
Total responses		**46**

keep their online identity private and also felt that their online behaviour was appropriate and did not require adaption. There was a strong sense of participants being very aware of the potential that inappropriate posting on social media sites might affect their professional identity: *My profiles are set to private, I am also very wary of what I put onto social networks* and ... *I think before posting a comment or picture on the internet* were typical responses to this question.

One key finding of the online debate was that participants indicated that they would use multiple SNS as Table 2.3 illustrates:

It appears that the more interactive SNS's are popular choices whilst the information hosting sites received a low response rate. Of the qualifying responses we received participants indicated that they would be keen to engage in a Twitter debate again and would use Twitter to engage with other organisations. Fifty percent of respondents did not perceive there to be any barriers to their using social networking services, of the remainder, 44% thought there were barriers, and 6% thought there may be. The qualitative responses are summarised as follows:

There was a reluctance to be open as there was the potential for misunderstanding, coupled with an awareness that some content would be subject to the judgements and opinions of others who had access and this would act as a barrier to using SNS.

Self-editing was important and assessing what was appropriate material to post on SNS was an on-going feature of using SNS. In essence there appeared to be a heightened awareness regarding the potential harm or risk which acted as a barrier to using SNS for almost half of the participants in this study.

The environment most effective in supporting participants learning included Blackboard/ GCUlearn (61%), self-directed study (43%), and social networking (50%). Qualitative responses all remarked on using Twitter: *Twitter is useful and has lots of information relevant to our course of study and interest and Twitter links to of various websites.*

Participating in the Twitter debate had an impact on the development of communication skills of 82% of the participants with 11% feeling that maybe their skills had developed. Participants also provided qualitative responses to this question which included statements about increased confidence and willingness to participate in online debates again, being able to actually use Twitter was key for one respondent here and developing professional language for another.

Responses to the question about using social networking services to communicate with service users were mixed with 50% saying no and roughly a quarter of participants saying yes or maybe. Participants providing a qualitative response to this question fell into two groups. First, for those who would not communicate with service users using SNS reason included, it being deemed to be unprofessional or inappropriate and the participants wishing to maintain professional boundaries: *I believe this may breach the appropriate boundaries of a social worker– service user relationship* and perceiving this form of communication to transgress and potentially cause problems. For those respondents who thought they may use it there was an emphasis on the benefits of these forms of communication for the service users, a recognition that a different account may need to be set up for this purpose, and comments about using SNS if it was deemed appropriate.

Almost all participants indicated that they would use SNS to communicate with other students or social work academic/practitioners and with agencies. Participants also stated that they would use SNS to access materials and resources which would complement their learning. The potential of using SNS for networking and making connections featured heavily in these responses.

The post-debate survey asked participants to identify if they would use social networking services in social work practice. Responses fell into several areas with participants being concerned about being tracked by service users or having their online profile available to service users. In addition some responses indicated that there may be conduct issues if online materials were not kept private. This response illustrates that steps are already being taken to review online profile information in practice: *Information is readily available. As a Residential Worker (Children) I have to monitor closely who is attempting to follow me.*

For other students using SNS was seen as a distraction which could interfere with studying. There was concern about maintaining professional boundaries and perceiving that SNS contact with service users would breach these. Several responses indicated that it would be acceptable to use SNS between colleagues. It was deemed important to ensure that personal information was kept confidential and a recognition that SNS could make a positive contribution as this response illustrates: *As long as you keep your personal life* concealed as much as professionally possible, SNS can be a really valuable attribute in social work practice and studying social work.

DISCUSSION

Student social workers in this study demonstrated an eclectic approach to supplementing their own learning with a range of SNS, and presented as being engaged with online learning using SNS in different ways to supplement their studies and develop a social work profile and identity. It is also apparent that the respondents in this study were able to take ownership of their learning journey using innovative and reflective strategies.

Twitter posts are restricted to 140 characters and this can sometimes act as a barrier to using this SNS as complex ideas have to be summarised and at speed, however this did not feature as a barrier in the survey responses which preclude participants from using Twitter in the debate. This may be due in part to the participant's familiarity with texting more generally and the use of mobile phones as communication devices as well as personal computers as discussed later by McKendrick in Chapter 5.

There was consensus about using technology and most students were already using SNS with only a small number not using any and this was in one case because of a negative experience. The induction programmes in both institutions emphasised the use of SNS and professional accountability for social work students and this appeared to have prepared students as their responses in the pre survey questionnaire demonstrated some critical reflection on how they used SNS and their profiles.

There were some key strengths and weaknesses of the design of the study. We achieved what we set out to do and hosted the debate between the two student groups, and collated responses from the online pre and post-debate surveys, however there were some technical hitches. During the debate at one study site the entire PC's powered off and we had to restart the machines. We would resolve this in future by having a technician available to advise us. We might also consider using a Twitterfall (www.Twitterfall.com/) to illustrate visually to participants what other students are contributing. There was a time delay between the student posting tweets and these being listed on the Twitter account on the screen in the classrooms and a Twitterfall system would show tweets as they were posted without the time delay thereby creating a more interactive environment. In future if we carry out this type of activity again we would ensure that we would set aside time for students to set up an account prior to the debate. Despite being given explicit instructions several weeks before on how to set up account not all of the students had set up a Twitter account and it took new tweeters most of the session to get used to the speed and methods of tweeting. The study team issued lots of verbal reminders to participants to use the hashtag so that we could capture the content of the debate. It took several hours of planning to secure dates when students would be available, and coordination of the sessions onto modules was also a lengthy process which we underestimated.

Overall there was a real willingness on the part of participants, evident in our analysis, to engage in SNS and adopt certain activities to supplement traditional learning strategies, particularly engaging with peers, practitioners, and social work academics. In this small scale research study our aim to involve social work students in an online debate was achieved and we are encouraged by the results which illustrate that this type of activity has enabled their learning and reflection on their professional development. It was also clear in the responses that students in this study recognised the ways in which their education and training is being supplemented by methods which are accessible and flexible. The results also indicate that messenger services are not popular. Messenger may be more suitable and popular with younger people rather than the sample here, and none of these messenger services are interactive or have the capacity to allow networking on the scale of Twitter or Facebook for example. Given that students appear to be making use of these SNS's to supplement their studies and aid their networking and connectivity skills, HE providers may need to attend to issues of value and quality of resources which are contributing to student learning outside of the materials which are delivered in the traditional classroom. HE's might consider the design and accessibility features of the VLE's to promote the interaction that students benefitted from in this research study. HE's should also invest resources in supporting teaching staff to make use of the interactive features of their VLE's in their taught sessions. Teaching sessions which encourage interaction between students using social media create a buzz and dynamic in a classroom or lecture theatre which is sometimes absent in traditional instructional environments.

There are several benefits which can be derived from encouraging the use of Twitter beyond the classroom in social work training and education. This small scale study illustrates one way in which students can be engaged in current social work debates and issues, facilitating the development of their professional identity. One area for future research is to better understand how practice educators engage with and use social media to support students during their practice placements. Only several years ago students were prevented from using mobile phone in classroom situations and it appears we have moved forward quickly to a position of encouraging students to interact with each other when in their learning spaces and a growing acceptance that social work students are benefitting from these interaction and new connections. Providers of social work education are well situated to encourage the appropriate use of these learning technologies and support the development of student's critical reflection which is crucial to their engagement with SNS professionally, in practice and in private.

3 Using closed Facebook groups to teach social work skills, values, and approaches for social media

Tarsem Singh Cooner

INTRODUCTION

Social media is beginning to play an increasingly important part in the way people are learning about each other and mediating their relationships in society. Before the introduction of the British Association of Social Workers Social Media Policy (BASW, 2012), the programme at Birmingham University, UK, had already started to develop practical approaches aimed at trying to ensure students left the course equipped with the relevant skills, values, and approaches necessary to practice in a socially networked society. Based on these experiences, this chapter aims to address three key areas. The first provides a rationale outlining why social work students should access learning about social media. The second illustrates how educators can use Facebook and enquiry-based blended learning (EBBL) to prepare students for social work practice in a social media age. The third uses students' and the author's experiences of the learning and teaching approach to assess its effectiveness in developing students learning about professionalism and social media.

BACKGROUND AND LITERATURE

With the growing use of social media in society the BASW Social Media Policy (2012) set out to clarify what it considers to be the professional responsibilities of social workers and students. As well as exploring risks for social workers and service users, there is also a recognition that social media has the potential to offer a number of opportunities for members of the profession to collaboratively develop their practice and find new ways of engaging with service users and carers. An excellent place to explore and develop the knowledge, skills and values required around social media use in social work is within the arena of pre-qualifying education. O'Connor, Cecil, and Boudioni (2009) argue that the goal of social work education is to prepare students for the challenges they will face in their future practice. This process of preparation should include opportunities to help students explore how the increasing use of social networking sites (SNS) within society has the potential to inform their future practices. This is an important area of teaching because research indicates that more people in the United Kingdom are using SNS to access information about others and enhance their social relationships (ONS, 2013;

Tsang, 2011). The Office for National Statistics in the United Kingdom for instance illustrates that 73% of adults access the Internet every day, this is almost double the figure compared to 2006 when comparable records began. They also outline that access to the Internet using mobile devices has doubled in the past three years and that a high percentage of those aged between 16 and 54 regularly use SNS (ONS, 2013). Ahmedani, Harold, Fitton and Shifflet Gibson (2011) also illustrate how using mobile devices connected to SNS via the Internet are becoming everyday methods of communication between most students. One implication of this mobile connectivity is that social networks created whilst at university can now be easily maintained once students leave. Because time and space no longer act as an impediment to the sharing of information and experiences, it is argued that students on professional programmes should be provided with spaces to reflect upon the potential implications of their SNS behaviours, particularly in relation to what they share, who they allow into their social networks and the image their social media profile portrays about them to the outside world. There are three common elements that SNS like Facebook possess: SNS allows individuals to 'construct a public or semi-public profile within a bounded system, articulate a list of other users with whom they share a connection, and view and traverse their list of connections and those made by others within the system' (Boyd and Ellison, 2007, p 211).

Because SNS like Facebook provide an easy way to connect people and view their information, social work education should prepare students to consider the ethical issues they as professionals (BASW, 2002; NASW, 2008) should be mindful of when engaging with these sites. There is evidence that some social workers have struggled to cope with the changes SNS have introduced, particularly in relation to accessing personal information and maintaining professional boundaries. Reamer (2009) for example highlights a situation in which a service user accessed private and personal details about a social worker through a mutual SNS friend. This resulted in the social worker feeling overexposed and unable to continue their working relationship. If the social worker possessed the skills to lock down their SNS profile, the issues caused by the above situation could have been avoided. Rafferty (2011) outlines a case where a student on placement at a leaving care project was encouraged to look up care leavers' Facebook pages to check on their well-being. It appears that neither the agency nor the student thought to gain the service users' permissions to access their information, nor it appears considered the ethics of their actions in relation to respecting service users' rights to privacy. Ayres (2011a) illustrates how a social worker was banned from practising after a conduct hearing found she had breached several professional boundaries, including befriending the parent of a service user on Facebook. These examples illustrates how social workers need to adopt appropriate approaches taking into account the fact that boundaries between private and professional lives have changed with the advent of SNS. There are also examples of the creative possibilities SNS offer to social work practice. Dale (2011) illustrates how SNS offer cheap and flexible means to encourage two-way communication between large numbers of service users and providers to develop better services. Ledesma and Casavant (2011) illustrate how Facebook can help social workers overcome issues of time and place to recruit, retain and provide support to foster and adoptive parents who may be spread over a wide geographical area. Cooner (2013) has demonstrated how SNS have the potential to allow students to develop and maintain communities of practice enabling them to share knowledge and experiences to develop their social work practice. These examples illustrate that the challenge for social work education is to provide students with meaningful learning opportunities to explore the possibilities and pitfalls that SNS present to their future practice.

Critical reflection

What opportunities do you think using SNS as an educational strategy presents in your current role?

COMBINING FACEBOOK AND EBBL

Facebook was used as a 'site for learning' within a Social Work Skill, Values, and Approaches (SWSVA) module with first year BA (Hons) social work students. Using an EBBL design, the learning objectives of the teaching were to enable students to become aware of the:

- changing nature of communication in society due to increased access to the Internet and social media;
- need for social workers to develop knowledge and skills relevant for a twenty-first century networked society;
- values social workers need to be mindful of when engaging in online activities, especially in relation to privacy, boundaries, and maintaining professional behaviours.

The rationale for using Facebook was to allow students to situate their learning within a realistic context by engaging with a problem they may face once in practice (Cree and Davidson, 2000). Using Facebook groups to resolve the problem enabled them to assess their current approaches to social media use in light of social work ethics and values.

Module background

The SWSVA module was created to meet some of the requirements identified by the Social Work Task Force's, Building a Safe and Confident Future Report (2010). This report identified the need for social work education to place a greater emphasis on preparing students to enter the workforce. It highlighted in particular the need for theory and practice to be integrated in teaching. The SWSVA module seeks to provide a foundation for the development of knowledge, skills and values that are essential for social work practice in line with the Professional Capabilities Framework (PCF). Given this focus, this module was the best place the locate teaching about 'Professionalism and Social Media'.

A short questionnaire at the beginning of the academic year revealed that of the 51 students taking the module, 89% (n=45) had an active Facebook account, 89% (n=45) accessed the Internet several times a day, 51% (n=26) felt they had the skills to protect their online personal data, and 59% (n=30) commonly used a mobile phone to access the Internet with 30% (n=15) using a portable computer. The online activities of this group were broadly comparable to those of wider UK society (ONS, 2013). The majority of students were already on Facebook and so an EBBL design incorporating closed Facebook groups was developed to explore issues of professionalism and social media.

Underpinning learning principles

Before outlining the specific activities students engaged in, it is important to provide a background to the underpinning principles governing the learning design.

Theoretical base – The EBBL design used for the Professionalism and Social Work sequence is based on a constructivist theoretical paradigm that acknowledges students bring their own personal history, knowledge and experiences into a learning encounter (Vygotsky and Cole, 1978).

Blended learning – refers to an approach that combines Facebook and face-to-face contact to stimulate learning through the processes of enquiry. The teaching approach draws on Garrison and Vaughan's (2008) three key elements which underpin effective EBBL designs:

- thoughtfully integrate face-to-face and online learning;
- fundamentally rethink the course design to optimise student engagement;
- restructure and replace traditional class contact hours. (Garrison and Vaughan, 2008)

Real life context – The EBBL design situated students learning in work related contexts (Burgess and Taylor, 2005; Cree and Davidson, 2000). Students worked collaboratively in teams to research, review, agree and propose solutions to the life-like problems posed by the tutor. The teams also had to present their work to peers and tutor and justify and defend their findings at the end of the learning process.

Enquiry – The enquiry-based nature of the teaching approach meant that a fundamental part of the learning emerged through the processes of dialogue taking place between students and, students and tutor (Vygotsky, 1986). For deep and meaningful learning to take place, Garrison and Anderson (2003) argue that students should engage in communities of enquiry. To enable this, the EBBL design used in this project sought to encompass the following elements into the online as well as the offline interactions:

- Cognitive presence – 'an environment that enables learners to construct and confirm meaning through sustained reflection and discourse in a critical community of enquiry' (Garrison, Anderson, and Archer, 2001, p 11).
- Social presence – 'the ability of participants in a community of enquiry to project themselves socially and emotionally, as "real" people (ie their full personality), through the medium of communication being used' (Garrison, Anderson, and Archer 2000, p 94).

- Teaching presence – 'the design, facilitation and direction of cognitive and social processes for the purpose of realizing personally meaningful and educationally worthwhile learning outcomes' (Anderson, Rourke, Garrison, and Archer 2001, p 5).

PROCESS OF THE EBBL DESIGN

The Professionalism and Social Media element took place over an unbroken sequence of six weekly one-day sessions. Five stages of this learning process can be identified:

1. Preparation – Prior to teaching, eight teams of six or seven students were created. They were given the role of a fictional social work team (identified by a colour). Eight closed Facebook groups were created for each team to allow the tutor to guide and students to share learning with peers (www.facebook.com/about/ groups). A hardcopy workbook was created to provide a roadmap and milestones as well as enabling students to record their learning.

Using closed Facebook groups – Before engaging with the learning design, it was important to get the consent of students to use closed Facebook groups. It was essential they did not feel worried or compelled to take part, particularly if they felt that doing so would lead to an invasion of their privacy. An overview of closed Facebook groups was given during the afternoon session of the first teaching day. It was made clear that membership of the groups was limited to the duration of the teaching. Students were assured that interactions in the closed groups would only be visible to the tutor and students (regardless of individual privacy settings). Also, students were not required to 'friend' their peers or the tutor to participate. Critically, this meant that Facebook based interactions could take place without participants having to allow peers access to their private social networks. The tutor as administrator was responsible for admitting members to the groups. Students without Facebook accounts were asked to create one for the duration of the teaching to ensure they could take part in the learning and become familiar with the interface, functions and privacy settings of a SNS platform. After the teaching, these students were free to delete their accounts. To promote team working and mentoring skills, Facebook users within the teams were encouraged to help non-users become familiar with the environment. If students had refused to create Facebook accounts, the backup plan was to employ a vicarious learning strategy within the learning teams (Mayes, Dineen, Mckendree, and Lee, 2001). No students refused to take part. The following section outlines the first set of activities students undertook in class.

2. Introduction and context setting – Students attended a full first day of face-to-face teaching. In the morning session students were introduced to the six-week learning design, the rationale for the topic area and the resources to support their learning. They joined their teams with the tutor ensuring non-Facebook users (6) were not overrepresented in any single group. The aim of the morning session was to contextualise why social workers should be equipped with the skills, knowledge and values required to operate in a social media connected society. To do this the following learning trigger and exercises described in Boxes 3.1 and 3.2 were used.

Learning Trigger – Students were shown the first 5 minutes and 55 seconds of an online video entitled '*Consequences*' (www.tinyurl.com/2ezaozm) created by CEOP (The Child Exploitation and Online Protection Centre). The story shows how a young man (Justin) uses social media to manipulate a young girl (Jade) into carrying out acts that will make her vulnerable to exploitation. Students were then asked to consider in their groups:

Box 3.1   Social work and social media – context setting exercise

If you worked with Jade prior to the events in this film, as her social worker:

1. *what knowledge and skills would you need to advise her about online safety?*
2. *how would you gain the relevant skills and knowledge to advise her about online safety?*
3. *what advice would you give to help her stay safe online?*

The video illustrated to students how open access to information like location services, pictures, SNS personal profiles, friend lists, home/school addresses, etc. could easily leave someone exposed to manipulation. The questions also allowed students to surface how their existing knowledge and skills could enable/hinder them as social workers in the process of advising Jade.

After a short discussion and feedback, students appeared to understand why learning about social media is important for their future careers. To explore this point further, the next exercise moved onto a more personal perspective. They were asked in their teams to consider the following questions:

Box 3.2   Making the learning personally meaningful

*Before your **first placement** consider:*

1. *How much information could someone find out about you by using social media?*
2. *If service users or future employers could see details of your (or your friends', family's etc) social media site(s), what image would that information convey about you?*
3. *What steps can you take to ensure you can engage in social media productively and remain safe?*

Given that the majority of students were already using Facebook, this exercise had a huge resonance because it related to their current practices and enabled them to explore some of the ethical, privacy and boundary issues they may not have considered before. These exercises completed the teaching for the morning session.

3.   Introducing the EBBL task – The aim of the afternoon session was to introduce and prepare students to carry out their EBBL tasks. To provide a real life context a fictional email was used to trigger the learning process. The context for the trigger is outlined in Box 3.3 and the trigger email in Box 3.4.

Students working in their teams were asked to look at the following exercise.

Box 3.3   *Setting a real life context for learning*

*You are a social work training team. Following the events with Jade, her foster parents have complained about the lack of **relevant advice** her social workers were able to offer to keep her safe. After a review of the complaint, your Director receives a report from the Complaints Panel with a set of recommendations. He sends these to your Team Manager.*

The following fictional email was used to trigger the student EBBL tasks:

Box 3.4   *The EBBL trigger*

Dear Teams

The Complaints Panel is concerned Jade and her foster carers were unable to get advice about staying safe online. The Panel has asked that I ask you in your teams to do some research and create four digital resources. I have allocated the teams below to create **one digital resource** for each group suggested by the Complaints Panel.

Team	Resource audience	Team	Resource audience
Red	Social workers	**Violet**	Social workers
Yellow	Parents/carers	**Brown**	Parents/carers
Green	Young people (8–11)	**Orange**	Young people (8–11)
Purple	Young people (12–16)	**Blue**	Young people (12–16)

You will be asked to present your digital resource on **Thursday 7th February 2013** in a **15-minute presentation**. In the presentation you must:

1. Introduce your resource and justify why the content chosen will be relevant to your target audience. (*8–10 Minutes*)
2. Present a reflective account of what the team have learned during the process and how it has/will change your future social media practice. (*5–7 Minutes*)

I have asked an academic member of staff from Birmingham University to provide the teams with support and advice using closed Facebook Groups.

I look forward to seeing your final work!

Good luck

The Director

4. Self-directed learning – During the next four timetabled sessions students had to use closed Facebook groups to engage in the development of a digital resource. Each team had to create a resource for one target group (social workers, parents/carers, young people aged either 8–11 or 12–16). The tutor monitored the discussions during this period and provided on-going advice and assistance. The aim of asking the students to collaboratively produce a digital resource directed at one group was to focus their research, dialogue and discussion during the learning process. The parameters and each team's focus for the digital resource are outlined in Boxes 3.5 and 3.6 respectively.

Box 3.5 Parameters for the digital resource

*A digital resource can take the form of a comic strip, short film, audio podcast, webpage etc. The resource must take **no longer than 5 minutes** to read, listen or watch.*

To focus their work, the following guidance was given to the individual student teams:

Box 3.6 Individual research focus

Teams Red and Violet

Purpose of digital resource

*The digital resource must offer some **top tips** for **social workers** using **social networking sites** like **Facebook**. The questions the resource must address are – how can Social Workers:*

1.   protect their personal privacy?
2.   ensure their online behaviour does not bring the profession into disrepute?
3.   maintain ethical boundaries with service users and colleagues?

Teams Yellow and Brown

Purpose of digital resource

The digital resource must offer some **top tips** for **Parents and Carers** of children using **social networking sites** like **Facebook**. The questions the resource must address are, what steps can Parents and Carers take to help their children learn how to:

1.   protect their personal privacy?
2.   judge what is and is not appropriate to say or post online?
3.   engage in safe online relationships?

Teams Green and Orange

Purpose of digital resource

The digital resource must offer some **top tips** for **Young People aged 8–11** using **social networking sites** like **Facebook**. The questions the resource must address are – what steps can Young People aged 8–11 take to ensure they:

1.   can protect their personal privacy?
2.   consider the appropriateness of what they share, **before** posting online?
3.   know what to do if there is online activity that worries them?

Teams Purple and Blue

Purpose of digital resource – Young people aged 12–16

The digital resource must offer some **top tips** to **Young People aged 12–16** using **social networking sites** like **Facebook**. The questions the resource must address are, what steps can Young People aged 12–16 take to:

1.   protect their personal privacy?
2.   assess when it is/is not appropriate to accept friend requests?
3.   seek assistance if they feel they are victims of cyber bullying?

To encourage an enquiry-based approach to their learning, there was an acknowledgement that:

> There are several ways to approach this task. The audience will be aware that there may not be a single correct answer to the above questions. Your responsibility is to

justify (during the presentation) the content you have decided to leave in, or leave out of your digital resource.

The aim of this statement was to ensure students did not restrict their creativity, research or approaches to accomplishing their learning task.

5.   Presentations – On the final day of teaching, all students attended a face-to-face session where they had to present their resource to their peers and justify why the content chosen would be relevant to their target audience. They also had to present a reflective account of what the team had learned during the process and what impact it would have on their social media practices. After each presentation, the audience had a chance to pose questions to the presenting team. The non-presenting students evaluated the digital resource and presentation from the perspective of social workers, parents/carers, young people aged either 8–11 or 12–16 depending on the team presenting. This approach allowed the different teams to see social media use from multiple perspectives. At the end of each presentation the students used handheld electronic voting devices to evaluate the presentations and resources. The TurningPoint audience voting system allows tutor's to use PowerPoint to display questions and response options so students using handheld voting devices can anonymously submit and have their feedback recorded (see: www.turningpoint.co.uk).

FEEDBACK AND REFLECTIONS

The feedback was collected after all the students had presented on the last day. The TurningPoint audience voting system (n=48) and evaluation sheets (n=48) were used to gather responses. The students' perception of their learning using an EBBL design was clearly positive across several areas.

Learning design

When asked if the Facebook element should remain part of the learning design for next year, 94% of students said yes with 46% agreeing and 34% strongly agreeing that they found tutor interaction on Facebook had helped develop their learning about social media and professionalism. In terms of the online and offline team work element, 91% of students felt it should remain for next year with 39% agreeing and 33% strongly agreeing that it had helped to develop their learning. In creating the digital resource 26% were not sure, 43% agreed, and 20% strongly agreed that it had helped to develop their learning with 88% stating that this element should remain part of the learning design for next year. In response to whether the presentations should be kept, 94% stated yes, with 62% agreeing and 29% strongly agreeing that watching peer presentations had helped to develop their learning. Also, 46% agreed and 39% strongly agreed that creating the presentations in their teams had helped develop their learning about social media and professionalism.

Critical reflection

If students are motivated to engage with these EBBL approaches what support might you need to draw on to develop them in your teaching/practice?

Meeting the learning objectives

The written feedback from the evaluation sheets suggested that students had found the experience of using Facebook to engage in learning about SNS personally meaningful because it had encouraged a number of them to change their online habits. These seemed to be centred on changing privacy settings, re-evaluating friends lists, and changing information on publically viewable profiles. A major learning point seemed to suggest students felt the trigger and life-like exercises had focused their learning and at the same time encouraged them to consider the impact of SNS from multiple perspectives. Feedback suggested students felt they gained valuable skills by learning how to work collectively in a SNS community to share knowledge and produce learning artefacts. This made some of them reflect on how they could use this medium in the future. This experience seemed to demonstrate to them the potential this approach offers to collectively problem-solve but also to be mindful of maintaining social work values such as privacy, confidentiality, and professionalism online.

REFLECTIONS

From an educator's point of view, the resources and the presentations demonstrated that students' engaged in a wide range of research to learn how social media and professionalism could influence their future social work practice. For students, having the space to create digital resources (such as videos filmed and edited with mobile phones, online comic strips, websites, online animations) allowed them not only opportunities for creativity, but also reflection around how the digital skills they possessed could be used in their future practice. Although there were minor issues that occur in any group work task, on the whole the feedback about the learning process has been very positive. Critical to its success was setting an appropriate context that enabled students to understand how the topic under study related to their current and future practice and using Facebook as a 'site for learning' seemed to vividly bring this point home. Students felt the learning approach enabled not only access to knowledge around social media use, but also valuable opportunities to learn how to develop skills in research, group work and digital literacy likely to play an important part in their future careers. The author hopes that the issues explored in this chapter will act as a stimulus to encourage colleagues to use SNS to build and share learning designs that enable students to develop the skills, values and approaches necessary to practice in an increasingly socially networked society.

Note: The above work has resulted in the development of the Social Work Social Media (mobile) app. The app allows social work educators and students to individually and collectively explore and discuss many of the professionalism and social media issues explored in this chapter. See appendix for further details.

When actual meets virtual; social work book groups as a teaching and learning medium in social work education

Amanda Taylor

INTRODUCTION

Practitioners involved in human services have a responsibility to understand the present and more often the past complexity within the lived experience of service users. Social Work Book Group is a method used to facilitate the development of this understanding, within the context of social work education, and is the emphasis of this chapter. The Social Work Book Group was initially established for first year undergraduate students in the School of Social Work at the University of Central Lancashire and was modelled on a traditional book club. At the meeting of the group students talk about the underpinning theories which explain some of the behaviours and motivations of the characters in the books they are reading. Students are involved in deciding which books to read and promoting the group using social media. The group is facilitated by a social work educator and usually an invited guest, either the author of the book or a social work academic with an interest in the subject of the book. As well as students, practitioners and teaching staff attend the book group either virtually or online.

Howard (2009), when discussing strategies to secure personal growth within the human professions, suggests that 'reading of fiction can help us broaden our awareness of how people from different backgrounds to us live their lives, what motivates them and why they hold certain opinions and beliefs different from ours,' she goes on to explain that, 'writers of fiction often explore areas of human experience that are often not discussed openly, such as the pain of bereavement or the destructiveness of envy' (p 24). This is consistent with the purpose of this chapter which aims to outline the educational and subsequent practice benefits for those who engage reflectively with fiction in a Social Work Book Group context; offering this approach as an accessible and formative learning tool, particularly for those who find reading academic material challenging.

The basis for understanding others begins with knowledge of the self. Howard (2009) states that, 'if we read fiction in a reflective way, questioning our own assumptions and attitudes, it can deepen our awareness not only of our clients but of ourselves and what motivates us' (p 24). Self-awareness is, 'the process of getting to know your feelings, attitudes and values and it is also learning about the effect you have on others' (Burnard, 1992, p 126). As a starting point for the development of personal growth we will consider how Social Work Book Group, a relatively new teaching method within social work education, can illuminate those things we may or may not know about ourselves and others. The development and processes involved are presented here alongside evidence of how it can complement the learning and development pertinent to social work education, as well as an exploration of its potential to prompt critical analysis and apply new understandings within academic and practice contexts.

Critical reflection

> *Are there any fictional books which you have read recently which might inform student social workers about a particular theory and help them to apply this?*

BACKGROUND

Social Work Book Group is a learning environment where students, academics and practitioners alike share interpretations, opinions and considerations of a fictional text in an actual and virtual space. It is a non-traditional and yet stimulating approach that facilitates the continuation of professional development at all stages of the learning journey. By the very nature of their configuration Social Work Book Groups advance knowledge, and this is due to the discursive and reflective manner in which fictional material is critiqued and reflected upon (Howard, 2009); and owing to the subtleties of being engaged in a groupwork type process (Clemans, 2011; Doel and Kelly, 2013). It is an experience that can lead to sophisticated ways of understanding, appreciating and connecting with what has been read (Scourfield and Taylor, 2013).

In addition, the process of actively annotating a fictional text affords group members the opportunity to contextualise the characters, the plot and sociological contexts as they evolve; akin to the unfolding landscape of the social work assessment (Milner and O'Byrne, 2009). The annotative process could be viewed as similar to that of the reflective notebook explained by Carter and Gradin (2001, p 7 cited in Bager-Charleson, 2010). This 'dialectic notebook' is described as: 'a tool for rethinking and reformulating ideas,' where the reader, 'will keep a list of important quotations, ideas, words, themes etc, together with page numbers, on the left hand side of the page' suggesting that the right hand side of the same page can be used as the reflective space (p 6).

The supplementary feature of technology, in the form of Twitter and Kindle, interweaved into the Social Work Book Group process aims to present students with an opportunity to develop their confidence and competence in relation to the safe and appropriate use of social media. It also provides a means through which they can become skilled at communicating more effectively in a public forum. A further advantage of the use of social networking is that it affords group members the opportunity to occupy a place within the wider social work population, potentially broadening professional networks as a result of being connected to what is essentially a 'community of inquiry' (Garrison and Vaughan, 2008, p 9).

Given the public nature of the digital platforms, access to learning that focuses on what it means to uphold public trust is shaped. It is this level of proficiency that can be cultivated through student engagement with a Social Work Book Group (HCPC, 2012; TCSW, 2013). Given the various unknowns that social media and social networking present it is crucial that students and early career practitioners have a technologically sound knowledge base. Student feedback indicates a substantial level of gain from an edifying exchange not only in the physical space but also on the digital platform. Commonality of interest in relation to professional knowledge, values and skills base engenders a sense of meaning and depth in the learning space.

The technological components of Social Work Book Group are a Twitter feed @SWBookGroup, a digitally storied chronology: www.storify.com/AMLTaylor66/the-use-of-book-clubs-in-social-work-education and Kindle reading devices.

A LEARNING SPACE FOR LEARNER EMPOWERMENT

Authentic learning spaces where the realities of practice can be explored often involve the use of biographies and case histories for the purposes of meaningful analysis and exploration. The use of this sensitive material in an educative setting, even though routinely anonymised, could be viewed as diminishing and devaluing the lived experience(s) of individuals, groups or communities. Despite this these understandings form the practitioner evidence base and it is from where a substantial proportion of explanations derive; otherwise known as 'practitioner knowledge' (Adams et al., p 92). By using fiction Social Work Book Group provides participants with an innocuous learning context as it is the lived experience of 'characters' that are examined to advance practice knowledge, contextualise practice values and revisit practice skills.

Crafting learning activities that cultivate critical reflection, analytical thinking and those which prompt revision within a knowledge, values and skills framework is the responsibility of the academic; whilst engaging with what Morgan (2013) describes as 'troublesome knowledge' puts an onus on the student or learner to examine beliefs, values and perceptions (p 220). Consequently, partnership within the learning space is key. It was as a result of the author's reflections upon student reading behaviours, the concepts of analytical reasoning and critical reflection that led to the evolution of a module based reading group which has grown exponentially, due to its overwhelming success, into a national Social Work Book Group.

The construct and format of module based reading groups operate on the same premise as a Social Work Book Group but are smaller in scale and subject specific, with reading material being drawn from the body of social science literature and research. It is the author's vision that Social Work Book Group will translate from the educational setting into the practice context. Given the nature of this multi-layered learning experience, within what is essentially a group work process, students and practitioners should consider how it could be adopted as a method of intervention. The creative possibilities within social work practice for book groups are infinite; employing this group work process across the broad spectrum of service-user groups, across the life course and in all areas of delivery could be revolutionary in many respects. It is a resourceful, innovative and original way of working that has the potential to engage individuals, groups and communities in a dynamic and effective manner in an attempt to facilitate change.

The success of Social Work Book Group is largely due to what Ryan and Tibury (2013) propose as, 'learner empowerment', which they explain 'addresses the challenge of changing the basis for interaction between educator and learner, to involve students more actively in the process of learning and thereby in the process of reshaping teaching and learning processes. Learner empowerment is underpinned by a drive to reframe academic relationships, connecting students and educators in collaborative efforts to recreate the 'intellectual commons' (p 16). The aims proposed by (Ryan and Tibury, 2013) are implicit features of book groups as a learning medium, highlighted by the diversity in the learning group or 'community of inquiry' (Garrison and Vaughan, 2008, p 9). In a Social Work Book Group it is students, practitioners, researchers, academics and occasionally authors who form and simultaneously contribute to the wider group discussion. Furthermore the value base underpinning this teaching method is clearly reflective of the social work value base if we consider the tenets that make it work; partnership, empowerment, commonality, inclusivity and collaboration. In the hands of a dynamic and creative practitioner a 'community of change' could be cultivated to immense effect.

SOCIAL WORK BOOK GROUP AS A REFLECTIVE SPACE

Despite its centrality within the curriculum, reflecting is a way of being that students often wrestle with and struggle to grasp; yet it is crucial to accuracy in case assessment and the subsequent decision-making processes. The difficulties alluded to are unsurprising given the copious interpretations of what critical reflection actually is (Trevithick, 2006). White et al. (2006) illuminate the complexity surrounding reflection and resolve it thus, reflection involves, '(i) a process (cognitive, emotional, experiential) of examining assumptions (of many different types and levels) embedded in actions or experience; (ii) a linking of these assumptions with many different origins (personal, emotional, social, cultural, historical, political); (iii) a review and re-evaluation of these according to relevant (depending on context, purpose, etc.) criteria; (iv) a reworking of concepts and practice based on this re-evaluation' (p 12). Alongside this Adams (2002 cited in Weinstein, 2008, p 4) suggests that it is, 'engaging with paradoxes and dilemmas' that can result in proactive critical reflection.

The development of the critically reflective practitioner lies at the heart of social work education. Bransford (2011, p 4) sets a theoretical context explaining that, 'the notion of "critical consciousness" was conceptualised by Paulo Freire (1997) as a step toward achieving praxis, or "critical reflection upon the world and action to transform it"' (p 42); in addition Sakamoto and Pitner (2005) explain that, *'the process of continuously reflecting upon and examining how our own biases, assumptions and cultural worldviews affect the ways we perceive differences and power dynamics'* (p 441) and that this results in, *'social workers learning to critically interrogate how his or her own identity has been shaped by the dominant ideology'* (p 441).

SOCIAL WORK BOOK GROUP: THE SOCIAL WORK KNOWLEDGE, VALUES, AND SKILLS BASE

When discussing the social work knowledge base we must be clear about what this concept means within the context of social work education and in terms of the practice approach; acknowledging the ever changing landscape characteristic of human existence and the social work profession (Worsley et al., 2013, pp xv–xvii). The profession in itself responds to societal change; however this is most often driven by the political agenda of the time. Trevithick (2005) articulates the function of knowledge in a social work context, if embraced from a systemic position: 'in order to acquire and to perfect a "toolbox" or "basket" of practice skills and interventions, we need to have a sound knowledge base from which to begin to understand people and their situations and to formulate plans of action appropriate to the circumstances encountered' (p 2). This illustrates the symbiotic and enmeshed nature of understandings and abilities essential for the social work student or practitioner engaged in education, practice, continued professional development and practice learning; substantiated by the requirements of both the Health Care Professionals Council (HCPC) Standards of Proficiency for Social Workers in England (2012) and The College of Social Work (TCSW) Professional Capabilities Framework (2013). Implicit in each regulating body is the stipulation that the development of knowledge, values, and skills is incremental and progressed throughout the career of the social work practitioner; and that the responsibility for this progression principally lies with the social work student/practitioner.

Worsley et al. (2013) have described the knowledge base as eclectic, citing this 'eclecticism as one of its [social work] strengths' p xvii). Social Work Book Group and the fictional content contained makes available a context in which the various types of knowledge, the range of values and the scope of practice skills that inform and underpin social work intervention can be explored, advanced and consolidated. It creates a space in which the elements of the social work 'tool box' can be connected in their entirety. All of the above are consistent with the influences of Bronfenbrenner (1979 cited in Cree, 2011) who offers a systemic model for the assimilation of understandings.

Critical reflection

Are there any particular theories in social work which you think would lend themselves to being discussed drawing on a fictional narrative?

In Social Work Book Group the deconstruction of characters, the analysis of the story and the interpretation of the sociological context, through the use of the social work knowledge, values and skills framework results in a thematic type discussion that could be compared to that of the social work process. Group members attend the learning space having read and annotated the text (information gathering), recount ideas they have constructed about 'who' the characters are (human development and psychological theory), what has 'occurred' (sociological circumstance and influences), and how they might 'intervene' (method of intervention, practice approach, values, and skills; underpinned by relevant legislation, policy, and agency procedures). Theory pertaining to human development, psychology, sociology, and relevant legislative contexts are appraised and understandings are conveyed. These elements of Social Work Book Group can yet again be likened to the way in which social work students are encouraged to think; making the necessary links between theory and the practice approach. A structure, for both the Social Work Book Group facilitator and group members, is offered below; one that aims to emphasise the significance of a coherent 'tuning-in' to the work (Egan, 2002, p 65), the social work process and one that raises awareness of how analysis shapes and informs a practitioners interpretation of the presenting circumstances (Box 4.1).

Box 4.1   Tuning and the social work process

Referral: who has been referred, circumstance(s), the referral agent, documented category of the case.

Knowledge base: age, life stage, gender, perceived identity, family construct, social background, race, ethnicity, religion, spirituality, education, employment (to include legislation and all set within a theoretical context); refer to Howe, 2009.

Client group: pre-birth, children, adults, youth work, older adults, sensory, mental health, learning disability, physical disability, brain injury.

Practice setting: community, hospital, residential, education, health, day-care, criminal justice (statutory, voluntary, private).

Assessment approach: questioning, procedural, exchange; refer to Milner and O'Bryan, 2002, p 53.

Method of intervention: outline the method of intervention: individual, group, family, community.

Practice approach: outline the practice approach (cognitive, behavioural, crisis, psychosocial, humanistic, task centred, and rationale for the approach taken; include stages of the work (beginning, middle, and end).

Skills: which were employed, how did they work; refer to Trevithick, 2005, p 82, skills inventory.

Value base: which were employed and why; refer to the origins of the professional value base (Biestek, 1957).

Care planning: outline the care planning process; refer to the classic text by Taylor and Devine, 1993, pp 41–69.

Implementation: approach taken to implementing the care plan; refer to the classic text by Taylor and Devine, 1993, pp 70–83.

Ethical dilemmas: outline any identified throughout the work and how these were addressed.

Evaluation: outcomes, what went well, what you might do differently next time, what have you learned.

Social work educators have a responsibility from the outset of the professional learning journey to make explicit the need for practitioners to grasp the reality of social work practice, and to understand that the lives of those who access services are often intricate journeys surrounded by uncertainty and change. They need to ensure that practitioners are equipped as well as possible to manage the flux and unpredictability of what they will encounter. Engaging with the book group as a non-threatening and informal teaching space is a creative method of supporting knowledge acquisition through analysis and reflections of a narrative as it evolves. It is within this learning experience that students can begin to safely connect with the actuality of everyday social work practice.

SOCIAL WORK BOOK GROUP: 'BRINGING LEARNING TO LIFE'

Having established that Social Work Book Groups have a place within social work education and that fictional works are the template for assisting students and practitioners to further understand and reflect upon the multifaceted nature of social work, it is now important to outline the elements of the Social Work Book Group as a teaching method, whether located within a module of learning, a reading group, as an online activity or a private study group; and to highlight their potential to replace, support, or complement some of the more traditional types of delivery in higher education. The construction of a Social Work Book Group within social work education requires some forethought and planning. What is also needed is the ability to consider and balance the overall teaching aims and influencing elements of the process from a systems perspective, to ensure that the session is focussed and results in individual and group level learning.

SOCIAL WORK BOOK GROUP PROCESS

Social Work Book Group (Figure 4.1) being the central tenet of the teaching method acknowledges the context but equally important is the attention paid to the range of learners, the fiction chosen and the environment created; as each one of these elements will impact upon and influence the other.

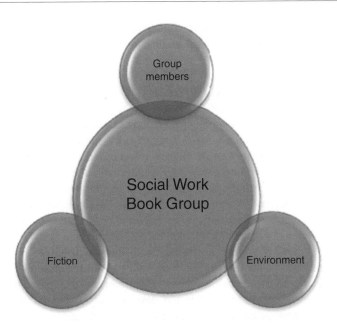

Figure 4.1 Dimensions of the Social Work Book Group in social work education

GROUP MEMBERS

An appreciation of who the learners are within the learning community, the stage of learning and the respective learning styles assists the facilitator to decide how best to balance the needs that exist within the group individually and as a whole. Kolb's 'learning cycle' which outlines 'experiential learning' (1984 cited in Mortiboys, 2011, p 12) and group work theory that cites 'common aims' (Brown, 1992, p 35) as the reason that groups should be formed in the first place are useful here. The potential for the cross-fertilisation of knowledge when the individual learners are at different stages of their learning journey is advantageous and can bring richness to the learning space. However, there is also a danger that the more dominant and knowledgeable group members will subsume those who have the potential to be silenced by the more confident and vocal contributors. Again, this is where the facilitator becomes significant to individual and group outcomes; skilfully fostering participation of all members will be crucial to the continuation of the group, the sense of belonging and the learning made available.

SELECTING THE BOOKS

How the Social Work Book Group chooses the fictional titles ranges from recommendations, to new releases, to the currency of the subject matter or the research interests of the academic facilitating the session. It is useful to have the student Social Work Book Group team review titles to screen for accessible and appropriate content and to eliminate those texts they believe that the wider student group would be less likely to engage with. Given that a Social Work Book Group is mainly located within the higher education setting the length and density of the texts should be acknowledged against the demands of the curriculum. A list of recommended reading is included at the end of this chapter.

THE LEARNING ENVIRONMENT

A Social Work Book Group as a learning environment requires the minimum of a room, group members, a text and a facilitator. A Social Work Book Group embedded within the social work curriculum attends to a number of levels of learning, development and progression. It begins with a 'community of inquiry' (Garrison and Vaughan, 2008, p 9) and can evolve into a much broader context known as 'communities of practice' (Wenger, 2000, p 4). On a basic level Walker (2008) discusses the need for social work students to, 'develop the habit of reading, and makes the point that this can be achieved through appraising 'novels or less academic books' (cited in Scourfield and Taylor, 2013, p 1). Furthermore, Mortiboys (2011) discusses the 'use of stories' as 'pivotal in gaining, retaining or indeed regaining attention' (p 56). This aligned with the essential skills required of social work students for academic success (Moore et al., 2007); and those which are transferable to the practice approach ie the development of the knowledge base, the ability to interpret narrative and the requirement to extend discourse pertinent to effective report writing (TCSW, 2012). Gambrill (2006) explains the role of knowledge, values and skills in terms of 'critical thinking' and states that they will ultimately assist with 'sound decision making' (xiii); all fitting with the central purpose of this Social Work Book Group in terms of access to a broad range of knowledge and the consolidation of learning.

Student feedback from the book group suggests that as well as developing their reading skills, students are able to think about and discuss how to apply theory with other students:

> 'reading a novel is a bit more relaxing than reading a purely social work book; discussing it means I got a lot more learning'

> 'book group helped me apply the theory I had learnt to practice situations'

> 'the novels chosen relate in some way to social work making it easier to apply the things I learn in class'

> 'book group is really innovative… I get to meet other students from other years and that hasn't happened before on my course'

Box 4.2   Social Work Book Group: A teaching and learning template

Who is involved: an academic lead, a guest speaker, a self-selecting student Social Work Book Group team, student tweeps (if choosing to include a social media dimension), social work students on all qualifying courses, across all of the years of study.

Participants engaged virtually, via a digital platform, can range from practitioner to professor and colleagues from across the health and social care spectrum.

Social Work Book Group leads will need to decide the context of your Social Work Book Group: module specific, course-wide, linked virtually to others or existing virtual Social Work Book Groups.

Location: a technology enabled teaching room or library space and the equipment to project the Twitterfall application (www.twitterfall.com) and the virtual space Twitter (www.twitter.com)

(again only relevant when engaging outside of the individual institution)

Equipment: Kindle, PC, iPad, laptop
(equipment only required if utilising technology to broaden the scope of the catchment of learners or connecting with other Social Work Book Groups/members who are unable to be in the physical space but still wish to engage with the learning activity)
Marketing: audience dependent: email; student VLE; student led Facebook; designated Twitter feed managed by both the academic facilitator and the student team

Facilitation: academic lead alongside a pre-arranged guest speaker/author/social work educator/social work practitioner
(a Social Work Book Group could also be used on a smaller scale or more personal level; in that it could be organised by students, practitioners or with any group of individuals that have a common interest in learning through the discussion of fiction)

Structure: a yearly planning meeting with the academic lead and the student Social Work Book Group planning team; book titles chosen; tri-yearly dates planned around the curriculum; facilitators approached (it is useful to consider research that links to the themes in the text chosen to develop the learning potential and promote engagement with current literature)

Learning Outcomes:

o   To appraise a fictional text drawing on social work knowledge, values and skills framework
o   To apply pertinent legislative principles to the fictional text
o   To consider possible methods of social work intervention; including practice skills
o   To critically analyse relevant theory and its application
o   To review research relevant to the themes arising
o   To identify individual learning needs and gaps in the professional knowledge base

Group process (actual and virtual): Social Work Book Group meets in a prearranged physical space to engage in the sharing of reflections regarding a prechosen text.

A significant feature of the co-ordination of the digital connection during an actual book group event is the role of what are known as tweeps; on this occasion student social workers who have volunteered to upload comments from their respective book groups onto the main @SWBookGroup Twitter feed. There is a main Social Work Book Group tweep who trains and manages all of the student tweeps across the participating universities and whose role it is to link the discussions on the @SWBookGroup Twitter feed via an application called Twitterfall.

The Twitterfall application is projected onto a main screen within the hosting university learning space and camera equipment for a live stream and recording are positioned to capture the session as a resource that is added chronologically to a Storify. Tweeting by participants within the actual Social Work Book Group space and from those students who chose to distance learn is encouraged. A hashtag #swbk is used to collate the tweets so that they can be viewed retrospectively as a learning resource.

Within the host space the academic lead welcomes the Social Work Book Group in situ and those participants located in various universities engaging from across the United Kingdom and elsewhere. The text is introduced; alongside the aims of the session. The Social Work Book Group guest facilitator then offers an overview of the fictional work, outlining the main themes arising from a social work perspective.

The guest facilitator then posits reflections for discussion. The Social Work Book Group is opened for discussion with main themes proposed. The academic lead manages participation both in the actual and virtual space; highlighting and making links to both research and practice. Furthermore, the lead academic grounds the evolving dialogue within the social work knowledge values and skills framework.

The session is brought to a close by the academic lead who outlines the main points that emerge as having been most challenging from the text and those which appeared to have generated the most significant pertinent reflection.

Additional thoughts and reflections are captured in a video blog: www.storify.com/AMLTaylor66/the-use-of-book-clubs-in-social-work-education

If understanding others is fundamental to effective social work practice surely then as a starting point is the need to begin with a consideration of the self. It is the level of openness within that self to begin to explore one's own life story, to reflect upon it and own it as one's own that results in a humanistic practitioner. As learners, personally and professionally, on a life-long journey of enlightenment, our readiness for learning will be essential to how we function eventually in a practice context. How we access that learning is being presented here, through fiction; as it is through the lives of others that we can discover ourselves. Therefore, as the contemporary philosopher Alain De Botton (2013) explains, 'good writers put a finger on emotions deeply our own but that we could never have described on our own' (Twitter, 2013); complemented by Bjorks' (2012) 'there are certain emotions in your body that not even your best friend can sympathize with, but you will find the right film or the right book, and it will understand you' (p 1). Consequently through unreality reality forms and we become.

SOCIAL WORK BOOK GROUP RECOMMENDED READING LIST

Ashworth, A (2007) *Once in a House on Fire*. London: Picador Publishing.

Axline, V M (1990) *Dibs: In Search of Self*. London: Penguin Books.

Barham, P (1997) *Closing the Asylum: The Mental Patient in Modern Society*. London: Penguin Books.

Brown, S (2013) *Breaking Point*. Martson Gate: Create Space Independent Publishing Platform.

Campbell, K (2013) *This Is Where I Am*. London: Bloomsbery Publishing.

Cherry, L (2013) *The Brightness of Stars*. Oxfordshire: Wilson King Publishers.

Cherry, L (2014) *Steering the Mothership. The Complexities of Mothering*. Spring Publishing, an imprint of CareerTrain Publishing.

Crane, S (1995) *'Maggie: A Girl of the Streets' & Other Stories*. Herefordshire: Wordsworth Editions Limited.

Donoghue, E (2010) *Room*. London: Picador Publishing.

Frankl, V E (2004) *Man's Search for Meaning*. London: Rider Publishers.

Horwood, W (1988) *Skallagrigg*. London: Penguin Books Ltd.

Joyce, R (2013) *The Unlikely Pilgrimage Of Harold Fry*. London: Black Swan Publishers.

Masters, A (2006) *Stuart – A Life Backwards*. London: Harper Perennial Publishing.

Morgan, D (2012) *Disappearing Home*. Birmingham: Tindal Street Press.

Peebles, S (2013) *Snake Road*. London: Chatto and Windus Publisher.

Rogers, A G (1996) *Shining Affliction: A Story of Harm and Healing in Psychotherapy*. London: Penguin Books Ltd.

Rowling, J K (2013) *The Casual Vacancy*. London: Little Brown Book Group.

Sapphire (1997) *Push*. New York: Knopft Doubleday Publishing Group.

Trigell, J (2004) *Boy A*. London: Serpents Tail Publisher.

Winterson, J (2012) *Why Be Happy When You Can Be Normal*? New York: Grove Press.

5 New technology in social work education: blogs and blogging

David McKendrick

INTRODUCTION

This chapter will focus on the use of new technological innovation in social work and in social work education: blogs and blogging. A blog is a derivation of two words, 'web log.' Blogs are written by individuals and then they are posted to the internet for others to read. Most blogs have a 'comments' section which allows others to post their comments and views on them. These new innovations may challenge both educators and students, although often their fears and anxieties about using these are similar. This chapter aims to explain these innovations and discuss how they are utilised by educators and students. The discussion which follows will illustrate how these innovations create and sustain interest and debates relevant to social work education and practice; provide examples of how these approaches promote reflection which is a central pedagogic and praxis feature of social work; and lastly explore how blogs can encourage students to become more active with a wider network of people in discussing the issues faced by the social work profession today.

In the context of twenty-first century there is a growth in internet access whilst people are mobile using smart phones, tablets, and laptop computers. The website Androids (www.androids.com/) reports there were over 285,000,000 sales of tablet devices in 2013 accounting for 50% of computer sales, with notebooks accounting for 33% of sales, and PC sales representing 17%. The *Business Insider* informs us that between 2010 and 2016 sales of tablet computers will grow from around 20 million to somewhere in the region of 400 million (www.businessinsider.com/). The International Telecommunications Union (ITU) predicted in 2005 that by 2010 there would be five billion cellular handsets that would be able to access the internet. In the same press release they predicted that by 2015 mobile access to the internet would exceed desktop access (www.itu.int/en/Pages/default.aspx). Recently, in a class I was teaching the students told me that none of them own a personal computer (PC) instead their computer usage was entirely from laptops, tablets, and smart phones. Internet usage is now mobile; the internet now fits in your pocket and you are never far away from it indicating that the ITU prediction was entirely accurate. Such unprecedented growth in new technology creates a change in the way students are engaging with learning and indeed how individuals are moderating their relationship with society in general. For educators and practitioners it becomes increasingly important that we re-imagine our relationships in light of technological changes that are taking place so rapidly and in such a diffused way.

One of the most obvious features of Internet 2.0 is the growth of social networking services. The proliferation of social media platforms has enabled users to become more active on the internet; users are no longer passive recipients of the web, rather they are co-creators making their own posts, producing videos, or taking photographs that they can easily share with each other, initiating interactions and networks between each other. Actor network theory (Latour, 2007) uses the ideas of 'nodes' to identify people within the network they inhabit, nodes are 'tied' to one another through their relationships. The increased diffusion of technology and the rapid growth in blogging, for example, offers opportunities for nodes to form new ties with other actors in the network. The nature of technology allows virtual relationships to become more powerful and have greater meaning as technology empowers the nodes to make wider and more sophisticated relationships. The internet through SNS has become a social space where friends, acquaintances, and strangers can share all manner of self-created content which allows for interactions from others who can express their opinion on what has been posted. The traffic this creates allows virtual realities to develop where participants can form relationships with others despite being separated by a variety of static features like geography time zones and social status.

BLOGGING AND BLOGGERS

Blogging (the act of writing a blog) has become a widespread activity and one which has grown in popularity with the development of the internet. Research conducted by NM insight (www.nielsen.com/us/en.html) shows that as of 2011 there were 181 million blogs in the world increasing from 36 million in 2006 with over 6.7 million people publishing blogs on websites and 11 million people using social networks to write blogs. This is a development mirrored in society as the internet brings us closer together increasing our connectedness and reducing the distance between all of us. As Marshall McLuhan envisaged in 1964 when developing his concept of the '*global village*'

> Today, after more than a century of electric technology, we have extended our central nervous system itself in a global embrace, abolishing both space and time as far as our planet is concerned.

(www.livinginternet.com/i/ii_mcluhan.htm)

The rise in blogging is a good example of this social aspect of the web. McLuhan's vision 50 years on is a reality as the web enables the formation, maintenance and cultivation of virtual relationships. Blogs allow you to commit your views and opinions and to have them published to the web. It is quick and simple and when published a blog is available for the world to see. Bloggers can develop large followings and are becoming increasingly influential in all sectors of life. One example of this phenomenon is the 'Never Seconds' blog written by Martha Payne, a ten year old child from Lochgilpead in Scotland, whose blog Never Seconds (www.neverseconds.blogspot.co.uk/) has raised £130,000 for the charity Mary's Meals which provide food for children in Malawi. Martha's blog was initially small; she photographed and reviewed her school meals. However when the local council, Argyll and Bute, decided to ban Never Seconds claiming that Martha's photographs of her school dinners could jeopardise the catering staff's jobs, her blog rose to national prominence. The blog's continued rise to global prominence has given the charity she has chosen worldwide attention and massive publicity.

Critical reflection

To what extent can blogging provide opportunities for social work students and practitioners to critically reflect on their practice?

Writing in an academic style is a challenge for many students, for those who are returning to education after a period of being away or for those coming to Higher Education from Further Education and can cause significant anxiety. Learning to write in an academic style can be intimidating and not everyone is able to recognise the need they have to build their skills in these areas and so it becomes easy to avoid developing their writing. Additionally academics are experts in their own particular area and reading their material can be difficult if you are not used to the language and terminology commonplace in academic textbooks and journal articles. A potential solution to this is for students to engage with the academic content of their course through blogs. As well as individual blogs, organisations invite guest blogs from academics and practitioner who discuss their research or practice see www.cypnow.co.uk/blogs and service users who can talk about their experiences for example www.mind.org.uk/information-support/your-stories. Blogs are often easier to follow and can help students begin to understand the complex ideas that they are learning about in a more relaxed and accessible format. A simple Google search of 'social work blog' provides 1.37 billion hits. The sheer size of this gives an indication of the variety available. Narrowing this search down to 'social work student blog' provides 514,000,000 hits.

Professional journalists have also capitalised on the potential in blogging. Community Care, Britain's professional social work magazine, has a blog specifically for students where social workers and social work academics recommend books for students to read www.communitycare.co.uk/blogs/social-work-blog/2013/08/the-books-social-workers-recommend-students-should-read. The academics are also identified by their Twitter name. The blog pages provided a tailored reading list as well as access to the academics and practitioners who are making the recommendations. The reading list itself is not solely made up of academic textbooks; other books including a monograph about the care system are also recommended. Students are introduced to the professional magazine, and the authors as well as a vibrant social work academic and practice community on Twitter.

The open nature of blogging promotes unfettered ways of expressing a range of opinions and views. These blogs provide an insight into the world of social work as it is practised today by those involved in the planning and delivery of services. Each author offers their own interpretation of the professional area they practice in and their opinions on the issues that face them in their daily work. Blogs are written and published immediately there is no editorial control; they expose the challenging aspects to being a social worker but importantly they also highlight the many positives and strengths of the profession. The act of writing a blog, even if the content is challenging to read, demonstrates the on-going professional commitment of the author. Their desire to be active and to express their views can be seen as a demonstration of their commitment to the profession. Bloggers such as Barefoot Social Worker (www.radical.org.uk/barefoot/) offer a contemporary personal opinion on the challenges, difficulties, and positives of being a social worker today, as well as commenting on current political and philosophical issues about the nature of social work. As with other blogs, readers can contact the author Hilary Searling directly to ask questions or respond to her blog posts, thereby forging new ways of developing networks.

Critical reflection

Do blogs provide a safe place for practitioners to examine the tensions inherent in complex professional environments? What measures would you take to ensure your blog was 'safe'?

Can you think of examples when blogging might be useful for service users/ carers?

CRITICAL THINKING

Reading a blog provides an opportunity to actively engage in critical thinking. The very act of seeking out information from this domain is a demonstration of a willingness to engage in some form of criticality. Blogs are a personal opinion and view of an issue, the existence of which encourages the reader to question and engage in a critical appreciation of the content of the blog. See for example this blog which is written by a social work practitioner who is highly critical of the bureaucratic nature of local authority social work in this post: www.hownottodosocialwork.wordpress.com. Social work practice relies significantly on the critical thinking capacity of its practitioners. Working in dynamic and evolving situations social workers are required to be critical friends to service users, they must provide a non-judgemental attitude and be willing to adopt a different viewpoint or opinion from others. This is a delicate role, working with people who are often experiencing exclusion, poverty and oppression can present real challenges the ability to think critically and the willingness to express oneself clearly and unambiguously is one of them.

Brookfield (1987 cited in Brown and Rutter, 2006) describes critical thinking as:

Thinking critically involves our recognising the assumptions underlying our beliefs and behaviours. It means we can give justification for our ideas and actions. Most important, perhaps, it means we try to judge the rationality of these justifications. We can do this by comparing them to a range of varying interpretations and perspectives.

(p 4)

Blogs provide a rich source of material to develop critical thinking skills. Blogs are often controversial; as in the blog example above they are one individual's view and can contain bias and opinion, sifting through others opinions encourages the development of skills in searching for material and reflecting on its content. Blogs provide social work students with the opportunity to begin developing these skills in a safe environment. Speaking up in a class of peers and expressing your opinion is not always easy and a carefully thought out well informed opinion is always valuable.

Social work students arrive on their course from a wide variety of backgrounds. Not everyone who leaves school wants to be a social worker; it is a highly politicised profession and involves a range of skills to deal with the complexity of human lives and experiences. The profession is not often positively represented by traditional media forms (Westwood, 2012) and yet this is how some students form their opinion of the social work profession. Some social work students may find the profession appealing as a result of their own personal experiences of social work. Social work students arrive on their degree programme with a variety of different experiences in their lives and for many the course is as challenging on a personal level as it can be on an academic level.

Social work students are required to demonstrate an understanding of the various theories and academic content of their course while at the same time identifying and questioning their own personal values. This questioning approach is often captured as critical thinking, a process where we deconstruct concepts that we had previously passively accepted, doing so in the company of others while using their thoughts and experiences as a tool to support us in our process. The next section considers the impact of particular academics who were pioneers in developing this kind of approach. All four registering bodies in Great Britain; the Scottish Social Services Council, The Northern Ireland Institute for Social Care, The Health and Care Professionals Council in England, and the Care Council for Wales all have clear statements on values and ethics all of which are similar and require similar commitment from registrants.

THEORIES OF LEARNING: FRIERE, SCHÖN, BANDURA, AND SEARS

The Brazilian educationalist Paulo Friere in his book *Pedagogy of the Oppressed* described the process of engaging with the experiences and understandings of others as a process of 'Dialogical education' where, by using dialogue and reflection we constantly redefine what we see our world to be. This 'world' is made up of the relationships we have, the people in our life and the places and spaces we inhabit. The proliferations of blogs that focus on social work are a significant digital addition to this process. This and the availability of the technology required to access the material provides the opportunity for a global appreciation of social work issues, themes and debates. Reading a blog, allowing it to inform your thinking and then adding a comment from your own perspective is a modern, digital example of engaging in dialogical education, it is also an act of developing your own network of people you engage with. The internet liberates us from the difficulties of time zones and geographical locations creating a more accessible world.

Schön (1983) describes the importance of students (of any subject) being allowed the space and time to reflect on their experiences and issues, by listening to others. The student sees the world differently, by critically reflecting on these new experiences and the student can reconstruct their own world and use the experience of others to support their own change. This requires people not only to 'hear' what others are saying but to 'actively listen' to the meaning behind it and to interpret this meaning for them. Schön offers the idea of 'reflecting on action', a process where a person reflects on action or actions that they have taken in the past and considers it in light of the current circumstances. This quote taken from The Critical Blog by Rebecca Joy Novell offers a reflection on action analysis about being a social worker:

> *Forget the bureaucracy, the paperwork, the unrealistic case-loads; at its core, you are doing a job which is led by your values. Not only is that rare, it is a gift. No office is perfect. In fact, the entire profession needs some drastic changes. Therefore, one of my new year's resolutions is to make suggestions and changes that will bring my office and my practice more in line with my values. I'm going to campaign more nationally for what I believe to be valuable social work.*
> www.thecriticalblog.wordpress.com/2014/01/13/starting-social-work-reflections-of-a-newly-qualified-social-worker

New Year is often a time for reflection and the author uses this space to enumerate the difficulties faced by the profession. Setting these against the core part of the job allows her to come to the conclusion that the job is more worthwhile than the difficulties it represents. There is a sense of personal and professional affirmation as the worker redefines their relationship with their work.

Social work education encourages students to see the incidents that happen in their lives not as static events but as dynamic opportunities to learn from. Reflecting critically and with the support of others provide a scaffold for this process, a carefully constructed learning environment that is well boundaried and safe can allow deeper expression and more developed clarity of thought. Social learning in this environment sees the lived experience of the learner as a vital and vibrant element of their learning.

This method of social learning was pioneered by psychologists such as Bandura and Sears and sits alongside the work of Friere and Schön in recognising the skills, knowledge and experiences of the learner as being central to their learning. Blogs tend to be succinct and generally well organised by the blogger, they offer an opportunity for students and those involved in either their university or practice education to examine specific aspects of the curriculum in a manner that emphasises a more social approach to learning, we all use the internet for a variety of purposes and learning on the internet offers a more familiar social environment for us all.

ACCESS AND AVAILABILITY ISSUES

Prensky (2001) introduced the notion of the 'digital native' to describe the learner born between 1980 and 1994 whose learning has been immersed in technology and who consequently are in possession of a greater knowledge and skills base than any preceding generation. While contested, as discussed by Thackray in this volume this concept is still quite useful. 'Digital natives' have been born into a world where mobile telephones, computer games and the internet has been an integral part of their life they have never known nor can imagine a world without it. When they are engaged in education, ICT skills are ingrained providing an advantage in negotiating this aspect of the learning environment. Alongside these digital natives are what Prensky describes as digital immigrants; those of us (like my colleagues and I) who have learned the language of the digital native and, consequently, we have a recognisable accent. Prensky provides the example of someone who looks for information in books first before turning to the internet as evidence of this accent which distinguished us from the 'digital natives'. Digital immigrants are disadvantaged in this respect as we have had to learn these skills as adults as opposed to being surrounded by them, for us this is something of a new environment while for the 'digital native' it is their natural habitat.

While there is debate over just how different these students' approaches to learning actually are it is generally accepted that young people born in this time frame do seek knowledge and conduct research differently preferring the internet or other forms of media to the more traditional academic methods. For educators it is important to recognise the characteristics of digital natives, or residents, and be sensitive to their particular learning style. We should not presume that accessing blog's and using blogging as a form of academic activity is as simple as it might first appear. While there undoubtedly is a proliferation of mobile devices with internet access and an obvious usage of these devices across society there are some barriers to using these devices to access blogs.

In my experience as a social work educator, there is a general enthusiasm for and excitement about the social work course. Students that I have taught have in the main, some experience of social work, usually gained through working in the field or through some personal or familial experience of social work services. This contact has often provided the impetus to develop their knowledge by applying for the course. The ability of the social workers they knew in their earlier lives to develop effective relationships, is often cited by students as a factor in their decision to study for a degree. There is a sense that these students are at the beginning of a journey and need direction and support to navigate their way to qualification. This is often tinged with a sense of trepidation at undertaking study at university level. The majority of undergraduate students on social work programmes need support from staff as they adapt to a new environment and a new peer groups. This can be compounded by the specialised and professional nature of the course; students who are registered with the regulatory bodies in Scotland, Wales, and Northern Ireland (social work students are not required to register with HCPC in England) often need support to understand the personal requirements that these bodies require of them and make sense of what this means for them and for how they behave and act away from their university course. Adjusting to the idea of being a 24/7 professional whose conduct away from the university needs to be of an acceptable professional standard is something that new students need time to adjust to. It is perhaps unrealistic to expect students, who are in this process of adjusting to the challenges of university life to be fully able to appreciate the potential for support that blogging and blogs provide.

USING BLOGS TO SUPPORT LEARNING AND CHANGE: ACTOR NETWORK THEORY

Blogging can provide students with opportunities to settle into university life and to begin to find their own individual identity as a student social worker. Students arrive at university through a variety of pathways. The requirement for social work to be a degree level occupation was made in 2003, meaning that social work qualifications were required to be taught at university. As a relatively new degree social work education has found a comfortable place in new post 1992 universities where there is an emphasis on widening access and encouraging students from 'non-traditional' backgrounds.

As outlined earlier in this chapter Latour developed Actor Network Theory to help understand how the individual (the actor) was engaged with what surrounded them (their network). In the case of students they can be seen as an actor in a complicated network that is made up of the various competing elements of their lives. The pathway for social work students is unique to each of them and will create different strengths and tensions for them in their life. For some these can be manageable and straightforward while for others the network they operate within can be a complex and challenging place. An example of this is from a student on one of our courses, for this student coming to university was the culmination of a long held ambition. However her family network was threatened by her extending her educational and professional network. There was a fear that the process of change she was involved in could create an unwanted space between her and her family. The academic and placement side of university presented only minor difficulties; it was the familial side of her network that was a challenge for her.

Students can encounter other challenges from the transition from their previous place (school, further education or work) to the new student environment. To provide support to students in transition at Glasgow Caledonian we undertook a series of interviews with students who had made the change from studying at school and college and who had been in the workplace. In these interviews the students identify their network, the world they exist within, and the hopes and fears they had about university.

The stories from these students provide us with examples lived experience of actor network theory as it experienced by each of them, each student had a set of concerns that are specific to them but understood and interpreted through their own understanding of the issues. For some these related to their own feelings of inadequacy and a sense of not being 'worthy' or 'good enough' to study at university. For others it was the environment and culture of a university that was something they were unfamiliar with (and to an extent suspicious of) while for others it was developing the skills to learn and contribute at university level that they were afraid of. Students can develop a critical awareness of their own situation then this ability can (with support) transfer to understanding the unique experience that people whom we work with have went through. Understanding how people organise and make sense of their world is a key challenge for social workers. Relationships are often complex and diverse and are mediated through a series of different personal, social, economic, and political factors that influence our lives. The wider the lenses your professional is viewed through the greater the chance of seeing as broad a picture as possible. Blogs provide an opportunity for exploration of these concepts or ideas and can contribute to our own acquisition of new knowledge.

Latour also examined the network from a technological perspective. The increased proliferation of technology affects us all it can provide significant enhancement to learning but we need to remember that accessing technology is different for everyone. For some, especially those digital immigrants or tourists, technology can be an obstruction and their lack of familiarity and experience may lead to feelings of fear.

There is a simple answer to feelings like these and that is to become more active, to engage with it, joining Twitter or Facebook is a simple task, most of these social networking applications are intuitive, there is no great risk to joining them, the challenge is to use them appropriately and professionally while all the time being aware that nothing that you post online ever goes away. Even if you delete it there will be trace somewhere. Social work educators need to explicit in informing students of this and be willing to support students in making adjustments to their use of technology to avoid difficulties in this area.

BLOGGING AS A SUPPORT IN CULTURE CHANGE

The reality of transitional experiences is that at the point of transition you are more likely to feel exposed and have feelings of isolation and vulnerability. Using Actor Network Theory can support us in developing an understanding of why students feel this way; they are out of their old network (home, school or further education) and are entering a new environment, one that for some represents a considerable challenge for them in terms of their families understanding of their motivation for doing so, the technological and cultural elements of the new environment are very different and this is experienced at the same times as feelings of vulnerability.

Latour casts this as developing new nodes in the student's network. Studying professional courses like social work have a practice element to them where the student operates in a professional environment undertaking specific tasks that may well be otherwise undertaken by a qualified social worker. Students need to demonstrate professional qualities and operate in an ethically acceptable manner. Students need to adjust to the learning, teaching and practice aspects of their course as well as the external pressures they are confronted with in their family and personal life. This was once memorably described to me by one student as 'keeping all the plates spinning'. Students can seek support for this from within the university from professional teaching, academic support staff or more likely their peers who are experiencing the same challenges and managing the same achievements as them. In these circumstances the students 'world can be limited and refer only to the other students in their own institution or those studying the same course close by. It is important to remember that there are social work is a global activity. Engaging with a global cohort of student needs the support of the technological aspects of the network that these students inhabit. Student social worker blogs are a vital part of this, increasing the sense of being joined up with other students. In this blog students from the NYU Silver School of Social Work offer their student counterparts in other countries an insight into social work as it is practised in America (see www.socialwork. nyu.edu/blogs.html).

CONCLUSION

This chapter explains how blogs can be used to support students studying for a social work qualification Blogs are accessible, the rapid growth and diffusion of the internet and the technology which allows access to it means we have internet availability more often and in more places than ever before. Blogging allows students an opportunity to engage directly with authors and this interaction can stimulate debate and discussion. Blogs are often written about real life experiences and provide a unique insight into these and the challenges the authors face. They are usually clearly written and can be brief and require little concentration or explanation, they offer easily accessible opportunities to explore the dilemmas and ethical concerns that are often prevalent for social workers. Encouraging student engagement with this activity offers an opportunity for students to develop their skills in acquiring new knowledge and engaging with the attitudes, values, and experiences of bloggers. Learning in this iteration, is taken out of the classroom environment and experienced in a more mobile accessible manner encouraging student to reconceptualise the learning environment as not being solely classroom or university based. Bloggers can often offer views or opinions that are not commensurate with the attitudes and values of the social work profession engaging in dialogue with bloggers allows students the opportunity to develop critical thinking skills and enhance their written communication skills. Although often challenging this is a significant opportunity to reframe learning and to support a new form of learning and engagement.

6

Creating #team turner: an autoethnography of connection within social work education

Denise Turner

HOW DID I GET THERE?

On a fine summer's day in July, I find myself facing a large audience as the middle speaker within a three-part Keynote presentation on social media, delivered to the Joint Social Work Education Conference (JSWEC). Amongst the spectators inside what feels to me at this moment like the Coliseum, are the great and the good of social work – academics and practitioners whose work I have read and admired for years.

My account of how a part-time, mature doctoral student, single-parent, and unlikely user of social media, came to find myself addressing such an auspicious audience will form much of this chapter. Whilst analyses of social media use within education, are beginning to appear more frequently in the literature, these are often concerned with the potential pitfalls (Allwardt, 2011; Bolton, 2011; Duncan-Daston, Hunter-Sloan, and Fullmer, 2013). Within this chapter, however, I will concentrate on the positive contributions of social media, particularly the social networking platform Twitter, and its value in building professional and personal communities, distributing knowledge, and reducing isolation.

I have chosen to write the chapter as an autoethnography, a methodology which mirrors social networking by both reflecting and connecting the personal inside wider social systems. Denzin and Lincoln (2003) position autoethnography within the fifth key moment in the history of qualitative research, alongside other innovative qualitative practices, which like social media itself, offer challenges to conventional academic traditions. Drawing from Richardson (1997) I have also interspersed the text with a series of 'scenes' in order to depict the very vibrant, lived process which led to my improbable interest in social media and my subsequent involvement with this, within social work education.

SMASHING THE MACHINES

When I began my PhD study in September 2007, I had been away from both education and formal employment for several years caring for my children, the youngest of whom had recently started school. Stepping into a campus environment for the first time since completing my MA in social work, twenty-three years previously, I was immediately made aware of how much had changed, by the students around me talking loudly into, or gazing at mobile phones. Irritably, I questioned what they could all be talking about and whether any of this mobile communication was actually necessary.

Winterson (1996, p 97) offers a description of her relationship to technology, which matches mine at this time:

> *The scientists say I can choose but how much choice have I over their other inventions. My life is not my own, shortly I shall have to haggle over my reality. Luddite? No, I don't want to smash the machines but neither do I want the machines to smash me.*

Like Winterson, although I would not have called myself a Luddite, I had nevertheless always considered myself to be part of the 'lost generation' technologically – those of us who left school and indeed university, long before mobile technology, computer use and certainly social media became widespread. This left me with a lingering mistrust of technology and an irrational fear that by pressing the wrong keys on any device I would somehow cause irretrievable global damage. My anxiety and feelings of incompetence led to irritability around technology generally and frequent outbursts to my children about how much better things were in the 'old days', before everyone, as it seemed to me, was wedded to screens.

Scene 1: family time (1)

> *Saturday evening at home – 'family time'. My children, Amy, Dan, and I are in the front room of our house watching a favourite television programme, or at least I am watching whilst they gaze at mobile tablet devices*

> **Me (irritably):** *Can you put those away please? We are either watching this programme and sharing family time or we may as well sit in separate rooms alone – or even go to bed!*

> **Amy (protesting):** *I'm just looking at 'Twitter' to see what everyone's saying about this – don't you want to know?*

> **Me (with a rising tide of further irritation):** *Twitter! No I do not want to know what's going on there! We've always managed perfectly well without it and I can see what I think without having to know what everybody else is saying… You're ruining family time … Please turn it off!*

> **Amy (sulking):** *I just thought it would make it more fun to know what everyone else is saying – if you looked you might think it was funny too*

> *Dan slyly pretends to take the moral high ground whilst slipping his iPod under a cushion and peering at it intermittently*

I explode with impotent rage and frustration …

Curtain

WORKING FROM HOME

Although my return to university was the result of starting a PhD, many of the financial, family and other challenges I faced throughout the process are shared by students at all levels of study (Collins, 2008). Initially, after so many years away from education I found both the academic requirements and the language difficult, particularly as I was combining these with the school run and other practical parental tasks. One minute my head would be swimming with Foucault, Barthes and Bourdieu, whilst in the next I would be helping to plan a cake sale, or searching for a lost PE kit. In the early days however, one of the most difficult and intractable problems I faced, was the isolation caused by working from home.

At this point, there was none of the support for doctoral students which appeared later on during my PhD process. I would visit the university to attend supervision sessions, usually on a monthly basis but apart from that there was little reason to be on campus and no office provision. The seminars and research presentations which were intermittently available to doctoral students, tended to be arranged for 4pm or 5pm, times which clashed with my parental duties and therefore attendance entailed complicated childcare arrangements.

Another social barrier was the subject of my research, which also required skilful negotiation at university gatherings. I had trained as a social worker during the 1980s and subsequently worked within various fields. However, my return to education was prompted by the sudden, unexpected death of my son Joe, in March 2005. Having been a social worker myself, I was both intrigued and bewildered by the behaviour of many of the professionals involved with Joe's death and my research was prompted by a drive to further understand this and the effect it may have on parents. However, before I began my PhD, I had not realised what a social barrier this line of research would be within many contexts, not least at coffee mornings, research workshops, and other networking events. During formal presentations of my doctoral work, it was common for people to leave the room in tears and so in other contexts I began to navigate around the subject, which limited my opportunities to discuss my research and thereby increased my isolation.

Scene 2: 'Something So Depressing'

A three day creative writing workshop for doctoral students from all schools and departments at my university. Participants entered the room nervously searching around for an empty seat next to someone who seems friendly. The workshop facilitator sits at the front – she doesn't look up as people enter.

Facilitator: *I would like you all to turn to the person sitting next to you and each spend three minutes talking about your research and what brought you to it*

I feel a rising tide of panic. Glancing at the door I plan my escape, but the young bright eyed man sitting next to me turns around with eager anticipation.

Young man: *Hi, my name's Justin[1] – do you want to go first or shall I?*

Denise: *Oh no you please really (attempting to delay the inevitable moment of embarrassment)*

Justin: *Well, I'm from media and film. I've worked as an independent filmmaker for a while and then I became really interested in the use and depiction of animals within films, so I'm exploring that within my research. I'm finding it really enjoyable. What about you?*

Denise: *(wildly contemplating telling him that my research is on global ballooning in the 18th century, I hear myself speak) Ah well, mine is a little different… I am in the Department of Social Work and well, I'm looking at what happens when a child dies suddenly and unexpectedly*

Justin: *(flinching) Oh really? Why ever did you want to do something so depressing?*

Curtain

#eswphd

By the time I reached the fifth year of my PhD research, much had changed within the university environment. The social work and education departments had been amalgamated to form a new University School and a separate University Doctoral School was established to meet the needs of PhD research students. Academic staff members were appointed within both the social work and education departments to assist and work with doctoral students. As part of these developments, I was asked to take up a new post, with the specific brief of supporting doctoral students within social work, particularly those who were part-time, long distance, in full-time employment or facing other barriers to effective engagement with networking opportunities.

Shortly after taking up this role I met with a fellow doctoral student to ask for his suggestions. I had known him for some time and consequently was aware of the challenges he faced with balancing parenting, full-time employment, and his doctoral work. I felt sure that he would have some useful input for me within my new post. However it was with some consternation that I greeted his actual suggestion of establishing a weekly 'live-chat' on Twitter. His idea was to use this as a way of ameliorating many of the challenges

---

[1] Author's note: The names used within this chapter have not been anonymised but consent has been sought and freely given in each case.

faced, particularly by part-time, distance, and other students trying to balance multiple roles. The weekly Twitter chat he proposed could allow students to 'meet' regularly in a space where they could discuss topics relevant to their research. He told me there was a weekly Twitter resource similar to this, which had proved highly successful, but suggested that ours be specific to education and social work.

Returning to Winterson's description of technology, whilst not wishing to seem a Luddite, I felt very dubious about this idea as I had hoped to provide some connection in the 'real world', rather than in 'intelligent space' (Winterson, 1996, p 97). However, regardless of these reservations I could see the potential in the idea – I just was not convinced that I was the person to carry it out. My doctoral colleague may as well have suggested I try open heart- surgery or joining the Space programme – I had no idea how to use Twitter and viewed it only as a modern conceit, which spoiled any opportunity for 'family time'.

It was with a sense of humility then, that I finally conceded and asked my daughter to show me around Twitter. Gazing at me suspiciously, she set me up online and demonstrated how to steer my way around my new account. Gingerly, as if it might explode at any moment, I 'interfaced' with a few others. After an initial pilot session involving myself and colleagues, most of whom were also new to Twitter, we held our first live 'chat' under the hashtag #eswphd. Whilst this helped me to further understand how the process works, we had a very limited response from 'tweeps', as I later learned Twitter users are termed.

Allwardt (2011, p 602) describes a similar lack of participation during experimental learning using a wiki, with social work students. One of her explanations for this limited interest was that the academic use of communicative technologies differs from personal use in one highly significant way:

> *Several months after the term ended, one student mentioned having difficulty with technology. The instructor asked how posting information on the wiki was different from posting information on Facebook or MySpace, which used essentially the same tasks of editing and saving. She replied, 'But we want to do that.'*

In the case of #eswphd, it seemed possible that people did not want to engage in an evening session with something work or study related, as Allwardt suggests. However, having taken the trouble to set up the chat and acquire some rudimentary skills I was not to be deterred easily. After a couple of weekly sessions, in an attempt to generate more interest I invited the Head of School to be a 'Guest Tweep'. He was already receptive to the benefits of Twitter and had used it to form contacts within the School prior to his appointment. His guest appearance attracted a few more 'tweeps' and I tentatively began to see the potential value of Twitter in advancing networking opportunities.

Gradually news of our regular #eswphd chats began to grow and although participation from our own students remained limited, there was a small but regular group of these engaging every week. Student appraisal from Allwardt's research (2011, p 602) demonstrates that 'although the Web 2.0 generation may use these applications in their personal lives, they do not necessarily want to use them in the classroom' and the experience of #eswphd seemed to support this. However, when discussing this with colleagues, within my university department, I was astonished to learn that another reason for the low participation may have been a fear of the technological skills needed to use social media effectively. This is supported by Allwardt (2011, p 603) who found that 'students also desired greater guidance with the technology. Not all students will grasp technological concepts quickly.' Having always assumed that a certain ineptitude with regard to technology was mine alone, I was surprised by this and even further astonished when I became identified within the Department as someone who had 'expertise' in the use of social media.

Scene 3: 'eswphd'

A Wednesday Evening at 8 pm, and I am sitting anxiously in front of my computer, as the time for the live chat approaches.

@DeniseT01: *Good evening and welcome to our weekly live chat. This week we will be discussing 'Living with chaos' this was suggested by @BennClaire. Thanks Claire*

No one else appears on the screen. I feel a sweat breaking out on my forehead. The entire enterprise is a disaster…I should have known… then suddenly

@lizit: *Hi there DeniseT01. Good to hear from you*

Suddenly several more 'tweeps' appear and the conversation is flowing so quickly I find it difficult to follow

@DeniseT01: *Please remember to put the hash tag eswphd on your tweets or they will get lost from the chat*

The hour passes swiftly and enjoyably – several new 'tweeps' appear and connections are furthered. I am in a glow.

@Paully232000: *Great chat. Remember to vote via the poll for next week's topic*

@gawbul: *Hi I've archived 162 tweets from this week's chat to the eswphd wiki*

@DeniseT01: *Thanks – you are both stars as ever.*

BUILDING A COMMUNITY OF PRACTICE

Discussing findings from her research on the use of technology with social work students, Allwardt (2011, p 603) writes that 'given the nature of the social work profession, one must also consider the possibility that some social work students simply prefer to work with people face-to-face.' Others, including Bolton (2011) warn of the potential pitfalls of social media activity for social workers, advising those in the profession that our conduct in virtual space is now as important as our conduct in every other part of our lives. Guidelines established by The College of Social Work, together with the Professional Capabilities Framework and Health Care Professions Council Standards of Conduct, Performance and Ethics, all endorse this, requiring social workers to maintain appropriate conduct, although this remains difficult to define both within digital space and elsewhere.

However, social work is fundamentally a profession of relationship (Sudbery, 2002). The Professional Capability Framework, devised by the College of Social Work (2012) advises that in order to be ready for practice at Level I, social work students should be able to demonstrate basic communication skills, the ability to engage with service users and the capacity to work as a member of an organisation. All of these skills require sound networking and social competencies and meet the human need to network. Bolton (2011) emphasises this powerful drive for connection as one of the key factors behind the success of social media, which allows people the freedom to form social relationships over greater time differences and distances than were previously thought possible.

In my own experiments with #eswphd, Bolton's description of human beings sorting themselves into groups and factions was clearly evidenced. Whilst participation from my own School remained limited, a community began to establish itself around #eswphd which demonstrated, often in inspiring ways, the human drive towards relationship, evidenced by the following examples:

As the live chats attracted growing attention, national Twitter users made various offers of assistance. @gawbul, a man I had not and indeed may never meet in person had the technical skills to archive all the posts for those who had missed the session itself, whilst @Paully232000 established a voting system for deciding each week's topic. Academics, including AMLTaylor66 and @JLWestwood both Senior Social Work lecturers from UCLan, also offered to appear as guest 'tweeps.'

At the pinnacle of our success with #eswphd @jonbolton who followed me on Twitter and occasionally participated in our chats, offered to help with establishing a website. This was to act as a host for archiving the weekly chats, as well as offering a 'blog' facility for interested parties involved with social work or education. Jon worked with @lizit, another supporter of #eswphd in establishing this website, for no gain other than furthering a community network of learning and mutual support.

Having spent much of my PhD process, feeling isolated and unable to make effective use of networking opportunities which often clashed with my personal responsibilities, #eswphd opened a new door into a world where people were actively interested in my ideas and in assisting with these. From feeling like a single mum with a part-time academic 'hobby' I also briefly found myself the central character in a Twitter support group, which Jon B dubbed #TeamTurner. As the last stretch of thesis writing loomed, members of this eclectic online collective would regularly urge me on to finish the last few miles in what felt at times like an academic assault course. Additionally, whilst my research subject had led to awkwardness in 'real world' social encounters, within the 'Twittersphere' I found myself able to reveal only as much as I chose. In social media participation it is possible both to 'hide' and indeed to exit all together, without drawing attention to oneself and whilst these activities may raise ethical issues (Mukherjee and Clark, 2012) they avoid difficult and embarrassing encounters of the kinds I had experienced in other 'real time' social environments.

Critical reflection

Can you think of an example from your own experience of using social media when you have decided to withdraw? What prompted this? How did this resemble or differ from a real life exit you would have made?

'A WORLD OF CONTACT AND RELATIONSHIP'

Writing about the ethical dilemmas posed by the growth of social media, Cain and Fink (2010) suggest that at the heart of these lies the problem of boundarying 'tweets' and other postings, which once published are available indefinitely to a global audience.

In my personal experience, the ability of #eswphd to disseminate information to a wider public in this way was only positive – reducing my isolation and increasing my confidence. However, as Bolton (2011) warns there are significant ethical difficulties within this, particularly for social work. Social work practitioners and students are accountable for their professional behaviour and the boundary between this and their personal lives, increasingly dissolves when, for example photographs from a drunken night out can be posted on the Internet (Bolton, 2011). Duncan-Daston, Hunter-Sloan, and Fullmer (2013) make a number of recommendations for addressing these ethical difficulties, including that social workers abstain from using social media completely. However, as Ayres, a prominent social media commentator states in a report for the Institute for Research and Innovation in Social Services (2011b, p 5):

> *If professionals working on the front line are unable, or not encouraged, to gain experience of the language and cultural norms of, say, Facebook, they are effectively disempowered from understanding and empathising with their increasingly fluent clients.*

Ayres suggests that non-participation in social media, creates a potential barrier between social workers and service users, and it may also increasingly prevent their own access to information and professional opportunities. Bochner (1997, p 435) writes of trying to bridge the distance between the 'academic man' and the 'ordinary man' in a manner which creates new forms of knowledge, capable of enriching practice. His description has much in common with the current dilemmas around social media:

> *The social world is understood as a world of contact, and relationship. It is also a world where consequences, values, politics, and moral dilemmas are abundant and central.*

From my own experience of creating #eswphd, professional use of this emerging 'social world' has the capacity to create exciting and innovative opportunities which bridge the gulf between the 'ordinary' and the 'academic.' Into this new space 'a world of contact and relationship' capable of forging pioneering collaborations and truly advancing practice is made possible.

My own encounter with such 'a world of contact and relationship' brings me full circle to the beginning of this chapter and my part in the Keynote presentation at the Joint Social Work Education Conference in July 2013. My memories of being invited to participate in this event are blurred, but I do remember at one point on Twitter, @jonbolton suggesting it as the germ of an idea which then seemed to morph into reality. Like many good ideas, it seemed initially unproblematic until I was faced with the looming prospect of addressing an audience who knew far more than I did, in almost every way. Eventually, I put aside my original plans to impress them with my imaginary encyclopaedic knowledge of social work and philosophy, in favour of speaking from the heart about my own experience, which as Frank (1997, p 135) describes, was the best I could ultimately offer:

> What if a group of professionals were to examine her and ask, what exactly do you have to teach? ... she could certainly say this and that but her true witness, the witness that 'really matters' ... is not what she could say but what she is.

Despite the encouragement and support my simple presentation received on the day, I remained troubled by lingering feelings that I had been audacious in undertaking it, due to my limited experience and academic status. A passage often erroneously attributed to Mandela, meaningfully meandered through my head during the days and weeks which followed the Conference:

> Our deepest fear is not that we are inadequate. Our deepest fear is that we are powerful beyond measure... We ask ourselves, who am I to be brilliant, gorgeous, talented, fabulous? Actually, who are you not to be?
>
> (Williamson, 1992, p 176)

In 'Fields of Play' (1997) Richardson, describes her often heavily contested attempts to re-design ethnography via a long narrative poem and also as a drama. Reflecting upon this she ponders upon the 'violation of safe space' between conventional academic knowledge and other forms and advocates for 'passionate scholarship ... where students feel "safe" to err, transgress, because there is space for tensions and differences to be acknowledged, celebrated, rather than buried or eaten alive' (p 186).

I have settled, for the time being, on viewing my unlikely inclusion within a Keynote presentation to such an auspicious audience, as part of answering Richardson's call. Keynote speeches within academic conferences are normally given by prestigious speakers. Therefore inviting a part-time doctoral student, speaking only about her own experience could be seen as violating the 'safe space' largely populated by academics familiar with talking to each other. Twitter, and other forms of social media offer the potential for violating 'safe space' in a way which, as Richardson suggests, encourages students to transgress, because of the gains they may reap from this. For me, one of the main privileges of attending and speaking at JSWEC was the collapse of boundaries between myself and academics I could never otherwise have achieved.

Critical reflection

What boundaries in your own professional academic or practice networks might be breached through your engagement with social media?

Scene 4: 'Inspirational'

(The auditorium at Royal Holloway, following the Keynote presentation by Amanda T, Jon B and me. Jon and Amanda were like firecrackers – I have the uncomfortable feeling I may have been a damp squib …. Harry Ferguson, Professor of Social Work at Nottingham whose work I have admired for years approaches …)

Harry: (extending his hand to shake mine, whilst looking me firmly in the eyes) *Denise … Inspirational …*

Denise: (turning in to 14-year-old schoolgirl – squealing) *Wow, thank you … do you know how much that means, coming from you?*

Curtain

HARNESSING THE POWER OF THE GENIE

The growth of social media invites unlimited possibilities for enriching communication and building networks. However these new possibilities are accompanied by challenges, ethical and otherwise (Bucher, Fieseler, and Suphan 2013). My own tentative excursion into the world of online social networking brought me undreamed of gifts and privileges. I moved from an often dingy mental place where working from home produced feelings of isolation, exacerbated by a research area that provoked awkwardness and distress, to co-creating and becoming part of my own 'Team Turner'. In addition, I forged networks and relationships with academics I would never otherwise have met or contacted and whose collegiality and support has enriched both my professional and personal life. I was also dubbed 'inspirational' by an academic whose work I had admired for years and given my own #Team Turner mug – a gift from @jonbolton which still sits proudly on my desk at work.

I am not naive enough to negate the potentially harmful relationships which may spring from social media activity (Duncan-Daston, Hunter-Sloan, Fullmer, 2013). However, like Bolton (2011) I believe that people are naturally social creatures, even without the technology and whether it is Twitter, or any activity which supersedes it, now that this social networking genie is out of the bottle, I do not believe it will be possible to push it back inside.

The challenge is to learn how to harness the power of the genie in a way that enhances both the social work profession itself and the work we do with service users. For myself, I found that the excitement I gained from Twitter was becoming almost addictive, eventually introducing 'an oversupply of possibly relevant information' and an invasion of work matters into my private life (Bucher, Fieseler and Suphan, 2013). I have gradually learned to temper this by judicious use of the off button, although this is not, of course, always as easy as it seems:

Scene 5: family time (reprise)

Saturday evening at home later that year – another opportunity for 'family time'. Amy, Dan and I are in the front room of our house watching a favourite television programme, or at least they are watching whilst I gaze at a mobile tablet device

Amy (irritably): *Can you put those away please? We are either watching this programme and sharing family time or we may as well sit in separate rooms alone – or even go to bed!*

Me (protesting): *I'm just looking at 'Twitter' to see what everyone's saying about this – don't you want to know?*

Amy (with a rising tide of further irritation): *Twitter! No I do not want to know what's going on there! If I can't go on it then why are you allowed? … You're ruining family time … Please turn it off!*

Me (sulking): *It's different – I'm just doing it for work. It's very important for me to keep up with what's going on you know- if you looked you might think so too*

Dan returns to the moral high ground, this time arguing that if I can go on Twitter then he should be allowed to go on his iPod, which he now slips out from under the cushion. Amy explodes with impotent rage and frustration ……………..

Blackout

Conclusions

Joanne Westwood

This edited collection has been a collaborative project which grew from a conversation and the ideas of small group of committed and enthusiastic individuals. In a little over six months the authors produced detailed discussions of their work and continued to revise and refine these. The contributions cover many issues related to the use of social media in social work education, but we do realise that there are several aspects which we have not covered in depth, such as social media use by carers and service users. We thus consider that this volume is our contribution to an emerging field of work which has the potential to drive forward new and innovative teaching and learning strategies which can be used and developed to transform social work education. We also believe that by supporting students to use these collaborative tools we are facilitating their development as practitioners who will be comfortable and confident users of social media in practice.

There are several themes which emerge from the projects and issues discussed in this book. This concluding chapter will summarise these and make some tentative suggestions and recommendation for how readers might take these forward into their practice as educators, researchers, or as social work students.

Using social media has been shown to be effective in reducing the isolation which students can experience when they first enter Higher Education. This isolation is not just experienced by first year undergraduates but also by PhD students as Thackray and Turner reflect on in their respective chapters. The potentials of social media to connect individuals and forge communities of learning is clear in the accounts of their involvement in debates, forums, and discussions about the progress they are making as well as in the works discussed by Singh Cooner and Taylor. The survey findings discussed in Westwood, Taylor, and McKendrick also demonstrate that connecting with peers and likeminded individuals would motivate social work students to continue to use social media tools in their studies to support more traditional learning strategies.

One key issue for educators, academics and practitioner's (and it is accepted here that there is often overlap between these roles) is the skill development needed to pilot and test new learning activities with students. What the authors in this edited collection have illustrated is merely the beginning of that testing out of new approaches to teaching and learning about social work practice, skills, and values. It is hoped by everyone involved in this project that our readers are encouraged to try out their own ideas and adapt some of the activities here for their own use. As discussed in the chapter by Westwood, Taylor, and McKendrick the Twitter debate which they carried out was modelled on their experiences of a debate on Twitter that they had participated in. They did not anticipate that the actual facilitation of this would require so much detailed planning and coordination, and was as such a steep learning curve for all involved, but a worthwhile activity for students who reported their enthusiasm for engaging in social media activities in the future.

Singh Cooner demonstrated how the closed Facebook project facilitated the development of a community of learning and allowed students opportunities to be creative in their approach, to engage with each other using an online learning space, sharing resources and reflecting on their progress. Providing students with spaces to do this involved the educator to moderate and monitor the discussions, and also to give feedback and encourage on-going reflection. The skills which educators use to facilitate learning in traditional classroom environments require some adaption to implement them in online learning spaces and an investment of time. Both Singh Cooner and Taylor in their respective chapters outline the processes involved in developing their projects and make specific links to social work theories as well as theories of learning. By providing this detail on the development and prerequisites for a closed Facebook Group and Social Work Book Group, these authors have thought carefully about the outcomes for students and how these link to regulatory frameworks for social work education. There are many other applications of social media in social work practice and it is hoped that readers are encouraged to try these out and share the learning and outcomes with the online communities of learning.

There are challenges to using social media and we should not underestimate the technological barriers which prevent or otherwise obstruct our engagement. If you are determined to try out activities and create an online presence using social media, the general advice appears to be to start slowly, observe what there people are doing, and familiarise yourself with the guidance on its use and on your professional profile. The BASW (2012) Social Media Policy is an excellent starting point for students, practitioners and academics:

> *BASW encourages the positive uses of social media for networking, communication and developing inclusive practice. Social media can enhance communication and be used as a positive tool in social work. BASW believes that good practice in social media is no different from that in any other form of communication. Social workers should ensure they maintain appropriate professional and personal boundaries and take responsibility for recognising ethical dilemmas presented by the use of different types of social media.*

(p 4)

In order for educators, academics, and practitioners to use social media effectively in their work with students and for the benefits of service users and carers, it is of course imperative that they are informed and confident in their use and application of social media. The authors of the chapters in this book did not start out as confident users of social media; Turner describes feelings of anxiety and disbelief that she is considered to be an expert. What these pioneers share is an attitude of acceptance that new technological innovations bring with them risks, concerns, and challenges but also potential.

Good practice and initial activities for academics may simply be setting up a Twitter account, and posting a tweet after a lecture to tell students who much you enjoyed their engagement and how you saw them making progress. If you are a student think about setting up a blog account which takes a few seconds, and write a short daily or weekly reflection on your experience of practice learning which might help you to develop your reflective writing skills which will be essential as a qualified social worker. If you are working in a social work team, you might suggest that social media is a topic for a discussion on your next away day, or at your team meeting. Simply raising the issues generates thinking and ideas about how you might use it in your practice. This might lead to a decision not to use it, but at least your team will have considered the benefits and disadvantages. It is likely that many of the service users and carers you work with will be using social media and for some this may be a preferred form of communication, how does your agency respond to this? Take a look at the Social Work and Social Media App which is listed in the appendix as this includes questions which workers and managers will be faced with about social media in practice.

There is little doubt that the development of social media in recent years has created opportunities for new networks and alliances in social work education and our contribution here is evidence of this. Had it not been for Twitter, it is unlikely that the authors included in this book would have met, let alone embarked on a project together. In doing so we all took something of a risk and in this case it has paid off. Not all of our social media activities have produced solid tangible outcomes and in some respects there does have to be an acceptance that this is a trial-and-error approach. What works in one context may not be applicable in another, and sometimes social media activities are short lived, there is less permanence about many aspects of social media, even though we are advised that everything online is permanent. This should not however lead us to lack confidence or willingness to try out ideas; it is this spirit of testing ideas which led to the projects discussed here.

GLOSSARY

Adobe Connect: is a web conferencing platform for web meetings, eLearning, and webinars. As well as providing for online collaboration this platform enables users to share and update documents. Ideal for discussing research, planning teaching between a module team and working directly with students: www.adobe.com/uk/products/adobeconnect.html

App: An app is short for mobile application. An app is an application software which is designed for smartphones, tablets, and other mobile devices.

Blog: A personalised website where you can blog (write) about your interests, ideas, opinions regularly and then share them.

Diigo: It is a multi-tool for knowledge management which you can use to highlight texts, collaborate, and share as well as organise information: www.diigo.com

Facebook: A social networking service that allows users to connect and share films weblinks, photographs, music, etc.: www.en-gb.facebook.com

Follower: The name given to a tweep who connects with another tweep on Twitter.

Friend: Is connecting with someone you know on Facebook.

Flickr!: Is an online photo management and sharing application which helps to share and organise photos.

LinkedIn: Is a global professional network launched in 2002 with 250 million members in over 200 countries.

Hashtag (#): This is a symbol, which is used to mark keywords or topics in a Tweet. It was created by Twitter users to categorise and store messages so that tweeps can follow the content of a discussion.

HEA – Higher Education Academy: Resources specifically for social work education: www.heacademy.ac.uk/disciplines/social-work-and-social-policy

JSWEC – Joint Social Work Education Conference: An annual event which brings together academics, practitioners, and service users to discuss and debate social work education: www.jswec.net/2014

Pinterest: Pinterest is an online tool for collecting, organising, and discussing information about people, places, and events which interest you.

Storify: A global social media platform which allows users to capture and organise online resources to tell a story which they can then post onto a social networking service such as Skype, Twitter, or Facebook: www.storify.com

Tweep: A person who tweets.

Tweep Up: An actual (as opposed to virtual) meeting of people who tweet.

Tweet: A short message (140 characters or less) which you can share with your followers.

Twitter: A global social networking service which allows users to network and communicate: www.twitter.com

YouTube: Is a social media platform which provides a global online forum for people to connect, inform, and inspire others using visual and audio media that instructs and entertains: www.youtube.com/yt/about

REFERENCES

Adams, R, Dominelli, L, and Payne, M (2009) *Critical Practice in Social Work* (Second Edition). London: Palgrave.

Ahmedani, B K, Harold, R D, Fitton, V A, and Shifflet Gibson, E D (2011) What Adolescents Can Tell Us: Technology and the Future of Social Work Education. *Social Work Education*, 30(7), 830–46.

Allwardt, D (2011) Writing with Wikis: A Cautionary Tale of Technology in the Classroom. *Journal of Social Work Education*, 47(3): 597–605.

Anderson, T, Rourke, L, Garrison, D R, and Archer, W (2001) Assessing Teaching Presence in a Computer Conferencing Context. *Journal of Asynchronous Learning Networks*, 5(2), 1–17.

Ayres, S (2011a) The Social Media We Need Not Fear. Professional Social Work. Retrieved 30 September 2011, from www.cdn.basw.co.uk/upload/basw_11730-7.pdf.

Ayres, S (2011b) The Future for Personalisation? Service Users, Carers and Digital Engagement. Report for the Institute for Research and Innovation in Social Services. Available at www.iriss.org.uk/category/resource-categories/reports?page=4. accessed: 30 November 2013.

Ayres, S, and HEA (2012) How Social Work Academics Are Using Social Media to Support Student Learning. HEA.

Barefoot Social Worker. www.radical.org.uk/barefoot.

BASW (2002) The Code of Ethics for Social Work. Retrieved 19 December 2011, from www.basw.co.uk/about/code-of-ethics.

BASW (2012) BASW Social Media Policy. Retrieved 23 October, 2013, from www.cdn.basw.co.uk/upload/basw_34634-1.pdf.

Bager-Charleson, S (2010) *Reflective Practice in Counselling and Psychotherapy*. Exeter: Learning Matters Ltd.

Bandura, A (1977) *Social Learning Theory*. Englewood Cliffs, NJ: Prentice-Hall.

Baym, N K (2010) *Personal Connections in the Digital Age*, Cambridge, UK: Polity.

Beresford, P (2011) The Guardian: Joe Public Blog: What Every Social Work Student Should Know: www.theguardian.com/society/joepublic/2011/oct/03/social-work-students-tips.

Biestek, F P (1957) *The Casework Relationship*. London: George Allen and Unwin Ltd.

Billett, S (2008) Learning throughout Working Life: A Relational Interdependence between Personal and Social Agency. *British Journal of Educational Studies*, 56: 39–58.

Bjork, G (2012) Bjork and books. Available at: http://theantilaugh.wordpress.com/2012/02/29/bjork-and-books.

Bochner, A (1997) It's About Time: Narrative and the Divided Self. *Qualitative Inquiry*, 3: 418–37.

Bolton, J (2011) Social Workers Must Be Cautious with Online Social Media. Community Care online. Available at: www.communitycare.co.uk/Articles/06/10/2011/117566/social-workers-must-be-cautious-with-online-social-media.htm. Accessed 30 November, 2013.

Boyd, D M, and Ellison, N B (2007) Social Network Sites: Definition, History and Scholarship. *Journal of Computer-Mediated Communication*, 13(1): 210–230.

Bransford, C L (2011) Integrating Critical Consciousness into Direct Social Work Practice: A Pedagogical View. *Social Work Education*, 30(8): 932–47.

Bronfenbrenner, U (1979) *The Ecology of Human Development Experiments by Nature and Design*. Cambridge, MA: Harvard University Press.

Brown, A (1992) *Groupwork* (Third Edition). Hants: Ashgate Publishing Limited.

Brown, K and Rutter L (2008). *Critical Thinking for Social Work*. Exeter: Learning Matters Ltd.

Bucher, E, Fieseler, C and Suphan, A (2013) The Stress Potential of Social Media in the Workplace. *Information Communication and Society*, 16(10): 1639–67.

Burgess, H and Taylor, I (2005) *Effective Learning and Teaching in Social Policy and Social Work*. Abingdon: Routledge Falmer.

Burnard, P (1992) *Communicate!* London: Edward Arnold.

Cain, J and Fink, J (2010) Legal and Ethical Issues Regarding Social Media and Pharmaceutical Education. *American Journal of Pharmacy Education*, 74(10) (2010). Available at www.ncbi.nlm.nih.gov/pmc/articles/PMC3058471 accessed 30 November 2013.

Carter, D and Gradin, S (2001) *Writing as Reflective Action: A Reader*. New York: Longman Pearson.

Clemans, S E (2011) The Purpose, Benefits, and Challenges of Check-in in a Group-Work Class. *Social Work With Groups*, 34(2): 121–40.

College of Social Work (2013) Professional Capabilities Framework. Available at: www.tcsw.org.uk/pcf.asp.

Collins, S (2008) Open and Distance Learning in Qualifying Social Work Education in Britain and the USA: Celebrating Diversity and Difference? *Social Work Education*, 27(4): 422–39.

Community Care. www.communitycare.co.uk/blogs/social-work-blog/2013/08/the-books-social-workers-recommend-students-should-read.

Cooner, T S (2013) Using Facebook to Explore Boundary Issues for Social Workers in a Networked Society: Students' Perceptions of Learning. *British Journal of Social Work, Early View doi: 10.1093/bjsw/bcs208*.

Crawford, K (2005) *Social Work and Human Development: Reflective Reader*. Exeter: Learning Matters Ltd.

Cree, V (2011) *Social Work: A Reader*. Oxon: Routledge.

Cree, V E and Davidson, R (2000) Enquiry and Action Learning: A Model for Transferring Learning. In Cree, V E and Macaulay, C (eds) *Transfer of Learning in Professional and Vocational Education* (pp 92–105). London: Routledge.

Dale, R (2011) Are Local Authorities Equipped to Engage with Social Media? *Local Government Information Unit*. Retrieved 22 May 2012, from www.blog.lgiu.org.uk/2011/04/equipped-to-engage-survey-results-from-130-local-authorities.

Davis, F D (1989) Perceived Usefulness, Perceived Ease of Use, and User Acceptance of Information Technology. *MIS Quarterly*, 13: 319–40.

DCFS, D D (2010) Building a Safe and Confident Future: Implementing the Recommendations of the Social Work Task Force. Retrieved December 12, 2013, from www.dera.ioe.ac.uk/876/1/dh_114251.pdf.

De Botton, A (2013) The Good Writers Put a Finger on Emotions Deeply Our Own but That We Could Never Have Described on Our Own. Twitter, 11 December. Available from: www.Twitter.com/alaindebotton. Accessed 11 December 2013.

Denzin, N and Lincoln, Y (2003) *Handbook of Qualitative Research*. California: Sage Publications Ltd.

Destinationsocialwork www.destinationsocialwork.com/Students.

DiNucci, D (1999) Fragmented Future. *Print*, 53: 32.

Duncan-Daston, R, Hunter-Sloan, M, and Fullmer, E (2013) Considering the Ethical Implications of Social Media in Social Work Education. *Journal of Ethics in Information Technology*, 15: 35–43.

Dunworth, M and Scantlebury N (2006) Blogging as a Reflective Journaling Tool. *Journal of Practice Teaching in Health & Social Work*, 7: 6–21.

Egan, G (2002) *The Skilled Helper: A Problem Management and Opportunity Development Approach to Helping* (Seventh Edition). Pacific Grove, CA: Brooks Cole.

Frank, A (1995) *The Wounded Storyteller*. Chicago: University of Chicago Press.

Freire, P (1997) *Pedagogy of the Oppressed* (Second Edition). New York: Continuum Publishing Company.

Gambrill, E D (2006) *Social Work a Critical Thinkers Guide*. Oxford: Open University Press.

Garrison, D R, Anderson, T, and Archer, W (2000) Critical Inquiry in a Text-Based Environment: Computer Conferencing in Higher Education. *The Internet and Higher Education*, 2(2/3): 87–105.

Garrison, D R, Anderson, T, and Archer, W (2001) Critical Thinking, Cognitive Presence and Computer Conferencing in Distance Education. *American Journal of Distance Education*, 15(1): 7–23.

Garrison, D R and Vaughan, N (2008). *Blended Learning in Higher Education: Framework, Principles, and Guidelines* (First edition). San Francisco: Jossey-Bass.

Geoghegan, W H (1994) Whatever Happened to Instructional Technology. Twenty-Second Annual Conference of the International Business Schools Computing Association. Baltimore, MD.

Gilgun, J F (2005) The Four Cornerstones of Evidence-Based Practice in Social Work. *Research on Social Work Practice*, 15: 52–61.

Health and Care Professions Council (HCPC) (2012) Standards of Proficiency: Social Workers in England. Available from: www.hpc-uk.org/publications/standards/index.asp?id=569. Accessed: 10 December 2013.

Howard, S (2009) *Skills in Psychodynamic Counselling & Psychotherapy*. London: Sage Publications Ltd.

Howe, D (2009) *A Brief Introduction to Social Work Theory*. Hampshire: Palgrave Macmillan.

Hrastinski, S (2008) What Is Online Learner Participation? A Literature Review. *Computers & Education*, 51: 1755–65.

Kirriemuir, J (2007) A July 2007 Snapshot of UK Higher and Further Education Developments in Second Life. Eduserv Foundation.

Kirriemuir, J (2008) The Autumn 2008 Snapshot of UK Higher and Further Education Developments in Second Life. Eduserv Foundation.

Kirriemuir, J (2009a) Early Summer 2009 Virtual World Watch Snapshot of Virtual World Activity in UK HE and FE. Virtual World Watch, Funded and Supported by Eduserv.

Kirriemuir, J (2009b) The Spring 2009 Snapshot of Virtual World Use in UK Higher and Further Education. Eduserv Foundation.

Kolb, D (1984) *Experiential Learning: Experience as the Source of Learning and Development*. London: Prentice Hall.

Latour, B (2007) *Reassembling the Social: An Introduction to Actor-Network-Theory*. Oxford: Oxford University Press.

Ledesma, K, and Casavant, V (2011) Enhancing the Reach and Outcomes of Child Welfare Programs through Social Media. In LaLiberte, T and Snyder, E (eds) *Child Welfare and Technology* (Vol Spring 2011). University of Minnesota: Centre for Advanced Studies in Child Welfare.

Lewis, B and Rush, D (2013) Experience of Developing Twitter-Based Communities of Practice in Higher Education. *Research in Learning Technology*, 21: 18598 – www.dx.doi.org/10.3402/rit.v21i0.18598.

Livinginternet.com www.livinginternet.com/i/ii_mcluhan.htm.

Luft, J and Ingham, H (1984) *Group Processes: An Introduction to Group Dynamics.* Palo Alto, CA: Mayfield.

Mayes, J T, Dineen, F, Mckendree, J, and Lee, J (2001) Learning from Watching Others Learn. In Steeples, C and Jones, C (eds) *Networked Learning: Perspectives and Issues.* London: Springer.

Milner, J and O'Byrne, P (2002) *Assessment in Social Work* (Second Edition). Hampshire: Palgrave Macmillan.

Moore, G A (1991) *Crossing the Chasm.* New York: HarperCollins.

Moore, S, Walsh, G, and Risquez, A (2007) *Teaching at College and University: Effective Strategies and Key Principles.* Berkshire: Open University Press.

Morgan, H (2012) The Social Model of Disability as a Threshold Concept: Troublesome Knowledge and Liminal Spaces in Social Work Education. *Social Work Education: The International Journal*, 31(2): 215–26.

Moritboys, A (2011) *How to Be an Effective Teacher in Higher Education: Answers to Lecturers' Questions.* Berkshire: Open University Press.

Mukherjee, D and Clark, J (2012) Students' Participation in Social Networking Sites: Implications for Social Work Education. *Journal of Teaching in Social Work*, 32(2): 161–73.

NASW (2008) Code of Ethics of the National Association of Social Workers. Retrieved 1 December 2011, from www.socialworkers.org/pubs/code/code.asp.

Never Seconds blog www.neverseconds.blogspot.co.uk.

Nielsen.com www.nielsen.com/us/en.html.

Northern Ireland Social Care Council www.niscc.info/content/uploads/nos_socwork.pdf.

O'Connor, L, Cecil, B, and Boudioni, M (2009) Preparing for Practice: An Evaluation of an Undergraduate Social Work 'Preparation for Practice' Module. *Social Work Education*, 28(4): 436–54.

ONS (2013) Internet Access – Households and Individuals, 2013. Retrieved January 8, 2014, from www. ons.gov.uk/ons/rel/rdit2/internet-access---households-and-individuals/2013/stb-ia-2013.html.

Orme, J and Rennie, G (2006) The Role of Registration in Ensuring Ethical Practice. *International Social Work*, 49(3): 333–44.

Prensky, M (2001) Digital Natives, Digital Immigrants. *On the Horizon*, 9(5): 1–6.

Rafferty, J (1997) Shifting Paradigms of Information Technology in Social Work Education and Practice. Critical Commentaries. *British Journal of Social Work*, 27: 959–74.

Rafferty, J (2011). Use and Application of Social Media in Social Work and Social Care Education. *Social Work/Social Care & Media*. Retrieved 1 December 2011, from www.swscmedia.wordpress.com/2011/11/27/ use-and-application-of-social-media-in-social-work-and-social-care-education-2.

Reamer, F G (2009) Novel Boundary Challenges: Social Networking. *Social Work Today.* Retrieved 3 December 2011, from www.socialworktoday.com/news/eoe_111309.shtml.

Richardson, L (1997) *Fields of Play: Constructing an Academic Life.* New Jersey: Rutgers.

Rogers, E M (2003 [1962]) *Diffusion of Innovations.* New York: Free Press.

Ryan, A and Tibury, D (2013) Flexible Pedagogies: New Pedagogical Ideas. Available from: www. heacademy.ac.uk/assets/documents/flexiblelearning/Flexiblepedagogies/new_ped_ideas/npi_report.pdf. Accessed: 15 December 2013.

Savin-Baden, M, McFarland, L, and Savin-Baden, J (2008) Learning Spaces, Agency and Notions of Improvement: What Influences Thinking and Practices about Teaching and Learning in Higher Education? An Interpretive Meta-Ethnography. *London Review of Education*, 6: 211–27.

Scantlebury, N (2008) Collaborative Learning Using Social Tools for Enquiry, Reflection and Sharing. *Distance and E-Learning in Transition*, 701–10.

Scantlebury, N, Brown, S, and Thorpe, M (2008) *Collaborative Learning Using Social Tools for Enquiry, Reflection and Sharing*. Lisbon: EDEN.

Schön, D (1983). *The Reflective Practitioner: How Professionals Think in Action*. New York: Basic Books.

Scourfield, J and Taylor, A (2013) Using a Book Group to Facilitate Student Learning about Social Work. *Social Work Education: The International Journal*, 32: DOI:10.1080/02615479.2013.832190.

Scottish Social Services Council www.workforcesolutions.sssc.uk.com/PfP/values.html.

Sears, R R (1951) A Theoretical Framework for Personality and Social Behaviour. *American Psychologist*, 6: 476–83.

Shrembi, A (2008) www.why-social-workers-need-toembrace-Web2.0.com.au. *Australian Social Work*, 61(2): pp 119–23.

Siemens, G (2005) Connectivism: A Learning Theory for the Digital Age. www.ingedewaard.net/papers/connectivism/2005_siemens_ALearningTheoryForTheDigitalAge.pdf.

Sudbery, J (2002) Key Features of Therapeutic Social Work: The Use of Relationship. *Journal of Social Work Practice*, 16(2): 149–62.

Thackray, L, Good, J, and Howland, K (2008) *Difficult, Dangerous, Impossible...: Crossing the Boundaries into Immersive Virtual Worlds*. ReLIVE08. Milton Keynes, UK: Open University.

Thackray, L, Good, J, and Howland, K (2010) Learning and Teaching in Virtual Worlds: Boundaries, Challenges and Opportunities. In Peachey, A, Gillen, J, Livingstone, D, et al. (eds) *Researching Learning in Virtual Worlds* (pp 139–58). UK: Springer and Open University.

Thackray, L, Scantlebury, N, and Thorpe, M (2007) *Evaluating Social Networking Tools to Support Professional and Practice Based Learning*. PBPL CETL Paper 15. Milton Keynes: Open University.

The College of Social Work (2013) Curriculum Guides for Qualifying Social Work Education. Available from: www.collegeofsocialwork.org/standard2colrhm.aspx?id=50&terms=Curriculum%20Guides. Accessed: 11 December 2013.

The Critical Blog www.thecriticalblog.wordpress.com/2014/01/13/starting-social-work-reflections-of-a-newly-qualified-social-worker.

The Guardian (2011) What Every Social Work Student Should Know, www.theguardian.com/society/joepublic/2011/oct/03/social-work-students-tips.

The Guardian (2013) The Club for Those Who Love Curry and Social Care, www.theguardian.com/social-care-network/2013/sep/23/club-for-those-love-social-care-curry.

Thompson, N (2002) *Communication and Language*. Basingstoke: Palgrave Macmillan.

Thorpe, M and Edmunds, R (2011) Practices with Technology: Learning at the Boundary between Study and Work. *Journal of Computer Assisted Learning*, 27: 385–98.

Thorpe, M and Gordon, J (2012) Online Learning in the Workplace: A Hybrid Model of Participation in Networked, Professional Learning. *Australasian Journal of Educational Technology*, 28: 1267–82.

Tsang, N M (2011)Ethos of the Day – Challenges and Opportunities in Twenty-first Century Social Work Education. *Social Work Education*, 30(4): 367–80.

Trevithick, P (2005) *Social Work Skills: A Practice Handbook* (Second Edition). Berkshire: Open University Press.

Turkle, S (1996) *Life on the Screen: Identity in the Age of the Internet*. London: Weidenfeld & Nicolson.

Turkle, S (2004) How Computers Change the Way We Think. *Chronicle of Higher Education*, 50: B26–B28.

Turkle, S (2011) *Alone Together*. New York: Basic Books.

Vygotsky, L S (1986) *Thought and Language*. Cambridge, MA: MIT Press.

Vygotsky, L S and Cole, M (1978) *Mind in Society: The Development of Higher Psychological Processes*. Cambridge, MA: Harvard University Press.

Waldman, J and Rafferty, J (2008) Technology – Supported Learning and Teaching in Social Work in the UK – A Critical Overview of the Past, Present and Possible Futures. *Social Work Education*, 27: 581–91.

Walker, H (2008) *Studying For Your Social Work Degree*. Exeter: Learning Matters Ltd.

Warburton, S (2008) *Six Barriers to Innovation in Learning and Teaching in MUVEs*. Liquid Learning. Available at: http://warburton.typepad.com/liquidlearning/2008/07/six-barriers-to.html.

Warburton, S (2009) Second Life in Higher Education: Assessing the Potential for and the Barriers to Deploying Virtual Worlds in Learning and Teaching. *British Journal of Educational Technology*, 40: 414–26.

Wenger, E (1998) *Communities of Practice: Learning, Meaning, and Identity*, Cambridge: Cambridge University Press.

Wenger, E (2000) *Communities of Practice: Learning, Meaning, and Identity*. Cambridge: Cambridge University Press.

Westwood, J (2012) Social Work and the Media. In Worsley, A and Mann, T (eds) *Key Concepts in Social Work*. London: Sage Publications Ltd.

White, D S and Le Cornu, A (2011) Visitors and Residents: A New Typology for Online Engagement. *First Monday*, 16.

White, S, Fook, J, and Gardener, F (2006) *Critical Reflection in Health and Social Care*. Berkshire: Open University Press.

Wiles, F (2010) Blurring Private – Professional Boundaries: Ethics and Social Welfare, Does it Matter? Issues in Researching Social Work Students Perceptions about Professional Registration, Ethics and Social Welfare 5: 1, 36 – 51 DOI 10.1080/17496535.2010.616114.

Williamson, M (1992) *A Return to Love: Reflections on the Principles of a Course in Miracles*. London: HarperCollins.

Winterson, J (1993) *Written on the Body*. Vintage, London.

Worsley, A, Mann, T, Olsen, A, and Mason-Whitehead, E (2013) *Key Concepts in Social Work Practice*. London: Sage Publications Ltd.

APPENDIX: SOCIAL MEDIA ACTIVITIES IN SOCIAL WORK EDUCATION

RESOURCES AND INFORMATION

Community Care the popular weekly publication for social workers has a blog written by @Kirsty_ComCare. The Social Work blog covers issues which are important to the United Kingdom's 2-million-strong social care workforce including pay and working conditions, stress, and social work conduct cases, see more at www.communitycare.co.uk/blogs/social-work-blog.

Destinationsocialwork is a web page hosted by Glasgow Caledonian University which includes contributions from student social workers describing their experiences of studying social work. See www.destinationsocialwork.com/students.

Gill Phillips aka @Whoseshoes tweets about her work inspiring change in social care. You can read about her work on her blog at www.whoseshoes.wordpress.com.

The online resource www.onlinemswprograms.com has produced a list of social media resources for social work education: www.onlinemswprograms.com/in-focus/resource-for-using-social-media-in-social-work-education.html.

Social Work Book Group is designed to support traditional teaching methods and further consolidate knowledge, learning and development within social work education programmes. Established by Amanda Taylor further information on the book group can be found here: www.storify.com/AMLTaylor66/the-use-of-book-clubs-in-social-work-education.

Social Care Curry is a network of enthusiastic curry fans that also love curry. They organise through social media @SocialCareCurry and meet up at venues across the UK to eat curry and talk about their passion for social care. Find out more at www.socialcarecurryclub.wordpress.com/about.

Founded by @Donna_Peach SOCPHD is a popular and fast expanding Social Research Hub which hosts blogs and discussion forums for a range of social science disciplines including Social Work, Social Health, Sociology, and many more, Find out more at www.socphd.co.uk.

Social Work Film Club @Studio66 was established to encourage discussion about how social work and social workers are portrayed in films. The screenings have taken place at the University of Central Lancashire for three years. Students, staff, and practitioners come together and watch a range of films from the social realists' tradition. For further information see www.storify.com/jlwestwood/studio-66-film-club.

Social Work Helper seeks to provide information to social work services about the challenges and barriers faced by service users and to encourage services to be more effective in how they deliver services using technology, see www. socialworkhelper.com. The SW Helper Storify contains useful ideas for how to use social media tools in working with groups and individuals: www.storify.com/ SWUnited?utm_campaign=website&utm_source=email&utm_medium=email.

The Social Work and Social Media App resource was designed by Tarsem Singh Cooner to encourage social work educators, practitioners, and students to engage with some of the difficult value judgements and ethical issues which social media raises for social workers and their work with service users. This short film describes in more detail how the App can be used in education and in practice: www.youtube.com/watch?v=_Vr6BLGdLcs. For iPhone or iPad go to: www.itunes.apple.com/gb/app/social-work-social-media/ id656114442?mt=8&ign-mpt=uo%3D4. For Android mobile devices go to: www.play.google.com/store/apps/details?id=air.uk.ac.bham.cooner.

SWAPBox manages and publishes your social policy and social work teaching resources on the web. As well as providing an environment for sharing hand-outs, exercises, podcasts, and videos, there is a forum for members to discuss resources and issues. Some of the activities included in this book are already available on SWAPBox see www.swapbox.ac.uk for more information or to register and start using this great resource.

This short film was designed to capture the views of participants attending the JSWEC 2013 conference: www.jswec.net/blog/conference-news/2013-news/flavour.

In this Storify Tarsem Singh Cooner describes the Facebook activities discussed in his chapter: www.storify.com/Akali65/combining-facebook-and-enquiry-based-blended-learn.

This Storify outlines how academics were exposed to an enquiry-based approach to help them learn how to create blended learning designs www.storify.com/Akali65/designing-for-enquiry-based-blended-learning-dibl.

In 2013 the HEA funded an event to engage social work academics with social media and other online approaches. This Storify captures the enthusiasm generated at the event in short film clips: www.storify.com/Akali65/feedback-from-the-changing-the-learning-landscape.

INDEX

Other Books You May Be Interested In:

Anti-racism in Social Work Practice
Edited by Angie Bartoli   ISBN 978-1-909330-13-9

Evidencing CPD – A Guide to Building Your Social Work Portfolio
By Daisy Bogg and Maggie Challis   ISBN 978-1-909330-25-2

Modern Mental Health: Critical Perspectives on Psychiatric Practice
Edited by Steven Walker   ISBN 978-1-909330-53-5

Personal Safety for Social Workers and Health Professionals
By Brian Atkins   ISBN 978-1-909330-33-7

Positive Social Work: The Essential Toolkit for NQSWs
By Julie Adams and Angie Sheard   ISBN 978-1-909330-05-4

Practice Education in Social Work: Achieving Professional Standards
By Pam Field, Cathie Jasper and Lesley Littler   ISBN 978-1-909330-17-7

Starting Social Work: Reflections of a Newly Qualified Social Worker
By Rebecca Joy Novell   ISBN 978-1-909682-09-2

The Critical Years: Child Development from Conception to Five
By Tim Gully   ISBN 978-1-909330-73-3

Understanding Substance Use: Policy and Practice
By Elaine Arnull   ISBN 978-1-909330-93-1

What's Your Problem? Making sense of Social Policy and the Policy Process
By Stuart Connor   ISBN 978-1-909330-49-8

Titles are also available in a range of electronic formats. To order please go to our website www.criticalpublishing.com or contact our distributor NBN International, 10 Thornbury Road, Plymouth PL6 7PP, telephone 01752 202301 or email orders@nbninternational.com